P9-AOV-710

ECONOMIC REFORMS IN EASTERN EUROPE

ECONOMIC REFORMS IN EASTERN EUROPE

by Michael Gamarnikow

1968
WAYNE STATE UNIVERSITY PRESS
DETROIT

Published simultaneously in Canada by Ambassador Books, Limited
Rexdale, Ontario, Canada

Library of Congress Catalog Card Number 68–11485

CONTENTS

PREFACE

The controversy over economic reforms has produced one of the most bitter intra-party conflicts in the communist part of Europe. This is hardly surprising. To any die-hard communist the economic system and its institutions are something much more than the mere problems of production and distribution. Orthodox principles of political economy are an integral part of his Marxist faith. Thus, any meaningful change in the traditional economic system means that he has to discard some of his most cherished ideological dogmas and to adopt economic concepts, which he has been brought up to regard as a cardinal sin. Pragmatic reforms may rightly be assessed by outside observers as the new suitable ideology in the era of goulash communism, but to a Marxist-Leninist they mean primarily the reversal of the basic tenet—the supremacy of politics over economics.

What to us in the West looks like a contest between outdated economic doctrine and pragmatic common sense, a dedicated professional revolutionary regards as nothing else but a mortal danger of revisionism bent on destroying a system true to the scriptures of the prophets of Marxism-Leninism. What is involved in the conflict over the reforms is not only the different methods of running the economy and contrasting approach to the basic problems of planning and management, but essentially a struggle of generations. The old party veterans, who learned their Marxist-Leninist faith when they were still a tiny minority group and to whom the doctrine still remains far more important than material opulence, cannot understand the feverish quest for rationality and pragmatism which obsesses the younger generation of party intellectuals, economists, and technocrats. Should material well-being be bought at the price of abandoning the one and only true faith?

For some fifteen years I have been watching these conflicts from the vantage point of my desk at Radio Free Europe. From the first abortive reforms of the short-lived 1953 Imre Nagy regime in Hungary, through the brief euphoria of the Polish Economic Model in 1956–57, to the bloc-wide pragmatic breakthrough in the mid-sixties. Long ago I became convinced that the outcome of the struggle between dogmatic sclerosis and pragmatic drive may well decide what kind of Eastern Europe will eventually emerge in the nineteen-seventies. For me this outcome is not only of academic interest, but it remains a life-and-death matter concerning some 100 million of my fellow East Europeans. This is why I devoted so much time to the study of the various aspects of economic reforms and their impact on the political and economic institutions of orthodox communism.

Anybody who undertakes a serious study of economic pragmatism in Eastern Europe is immediately confronted by the same problem which effectively frustrated the builders of the Tower of Babel. The available research material—mainly theoretical articles, decrees and resolutions of official bodies, and statements of Party leaders—are published in not less than ten different languages. Even a superhuman linguist cannot possibly master all the available material in its original form, much less separate the grain from the chaff. Here my membership in Radio Free Europe, with its daily analytical reviews of East European events and a multinational research department, has proven to be a great advantage. Important happenings in my chosen field were brought to my attention almost as soon as they occurred. I was briefed about any significant theoretical article as soon as it became available and a few days later I would study the text in the English translation. Last, but not least, I had the benefit of reading hundreds of research papers and situation reports produced by my colleagues of other nationalities. Many of them helped me actively in preparing this book for publication by checking the original references and filling the gaps in my factual material. To all of them I wish to express my sincere gratitude.

This book is based on a series of articles which were published in *East Europe*, 1964–67. As a matter of fact, it was the editor of *East Europe* who first encouraged me to undertake a broad comparative study of economic reforms throughout the Moscow bloc. The public response to those articles has been very gratifying (including a surprisingly positive review of one of them in the Czech regime periodical *Kulturni Tvorba*) and this has encouraged me to enlarge and update the material contained in those articles into the more comprehensive form of a book.

Of sheer necessity this is simply an interim report on economic reforms in Eastern Europe, a movement which has just started gathering momentum. Any attempt to make a static exposition of a dynamic phenomenon is a truly frustrating experience. Often when I was rewriting the text to accommodate a new development, I wished I had been writing about ancient Greek history. The publishers and I have made every effort to keep the reader up to date. If here and there we were overtaken by events, this is the inevitable price of the publishing schedules.

I regret that I was not always able to take cognizance of the fact that several persons to whom I refer and whom I cite have passed away in the interim between writing and publication.

Now a word or two about the sources. As already stated, I have studied the bulk of available material in translation. For this reason I have decided not to reproduce the titles of the articles I quote, as references or in footnotes, in the original language. To do so could give the reader a false impression of bogus authenticity. I prefer therefore to use a title which is a literal translation of the original. It may be a minor matter but I want to keep the record straight. For the sake of uniformity I have used the same translated titles for the material I have studied in the original language.

I hope I may be permitted to end this preface on a personal note. This book is in essence a spare-time effort. Most of it was written in the evening and during weekends when my regular duties were done. The chief victim has been my wife who was, to coin a phrase, "a book widow" for many months. Throughout all this time she showed the greatest possible degree of tolerance and understanding. As a token of my appreciation I would like to dedicate this book to her.

M. G.

1

★

MARXIST ECONOMIC THINKING IN A MELTING POT

A specter is haunting Eastern Europe, the specter of economic revisionism. This paraphrase of the opening sentence of the *Communist Manifesto* provides a very accurate description of the intense intellectual ferment which has characterized economic thinking throughout the Soviet bloc since the middle nineteen-fifties. Traditional economic theories, time-honored dogmas, and old established practices of planning and industrial management are not only openly challenged, but publicly condemned as "unworkable and hampering further economic progress" (47).[1] From Titoist Yugoslavia to a near-Stalinist East Germany and from pragmatic Poland to traditionalist Bulgaria—everywhere we are witnessing a frantic search for an alternative economic system to replace the outdated methods of running the national economy. The reasons for this outbreak of economic pragmatism are not hard to find. For more than a decade the whole Moscow bloc has been passing through a phase of persistent economic difficulties, due to anachronistic methods of planning and inefficient and often inept management.

But the root of the trouble goes much deeper than the mere frustration with old methods of planning and practices of management. The crux of the matter is that all thinking economists and some of the more intelligent party politicians in the Soviet bloc have lost faith in the validity of the standard economic teach-

---

[1] The reference number is to the Bibliography of Works Cited at the end of this book.

ings of Marxism-Leninism. The basic implication underlying all this revisionist ferment is a tacit admission that traditional theories of Marxism-Leninism and its accepted practical solutions—developed in completely different political, economic, and social conditions—"no longer reflect the realities of a modern industrial society" (140). The fallacy of old dogmas is shown up every day by statistical evidence and economic facts.

It is not an exaggeration to say that Marxist economic thinking throughout the Soviet bloc is today in a state of deep crisis. The source of this has been diagnosed by some Polish economists as a basic contradiction between the old methods of economic planning and industrial management, evolved at another stage of economic development, and the current aims of economic policy, as determined by an objective need to substitute intensive forms of promoting economic growth for the traditional extensive ones (172, pp. 66–77).

As communist economies began to emerge from the era of absolute scarcity and strictly controlled production and distribution into a stage of a limited buyers' market, the orthodox centralist system of planning and industrial management by an *a priori* determination of economic priorities inevitably began to break down. The rate of economic growth began to fall and could only be maintained at its present level by excessive new investment, whereas the basic requirement is that of a higher productivity of the existing economic potential (143). Production tended to lose touch with the actual market requirements, resulting in huge accumulation of unwanted stocks.[2]

Given the centralist planning system this process was inevitable, since the communist economies are now in transition from an era of a predominantly investment demand, determined by the planners themselves, to a period of a predominantly consumer demand, determined by far less easily predictable aggregate requirements,

---

[2] In Poland, for instance, in 1963 for every 1 per cent growth of global output there was a 2.7 per cent increase in unwanted stocks (*Zycie Gospodarcze* [January 21, 1964]). In 1964 the stocks increased by a further 8.9 per cent over the 1963 level (*Ibid.* [January 3, 1965]), and in 1965 they were 11 per cent higher than in 1964 (*Ibid.*, [January 9, 1966]). In 1966 for every 1 per cent of the growth in output there was a 1.65 per cent growth in stocks (*Ibid.* [March 5, 1967]).

desires, and even caprices of the mass of the population. This effective consumer demand did not exert much weight at the stage of absolute scarcities, when practically everything which was being produced for internal consumption, was sure to be bought. But even in a limited buyers market the situation is completely different. At the same time, the existing system provides no incentive to the producers to adapt their output to the effective demand, as determined by the real needs of either industrial or consumer customers. (144). Among other harmful effects, this results in the pernicious phenomenon of "overproduction of unsaleable and unwanted goods in the midst of still prevailing scarcity."

Orthodox Marxist political economy is simply unable either to provide a theoretical explanation for all this waste and the growing economic disproportions, or still more to suggest an effective set of remedies (33). The whole problem is aggravated by the fact that, as a rule, the political leaders of the individual communist parties are so steeped in the old ideas of economic dogmatism that they are unable either to evolve the correct way out of the growing contradictions within the existing economic system, or even to accept rational suggestions put forward by many of their own economists.

This does not mean that there is no acute awareness of the magnitude of the existing problem, both within the highest party echelons and particularly among the younger generation of economists, managers, technocrats, and other members of the intelligentsia and managerial class. But the party leaders are afraid to put into effect anything beyond the half-way palliatives, and the younger generation has as yet no real voice in formulating the economic policy of the communist state.

Nevertheless there is a constant search going on in all more advanced communist countries, the essential objective of which is to spot the flaws in the economic theories and practices of orthodox Marxist political economy, to suggest effective remedies, and to bring the theory of planning up to date. At the same time, concrete measures are being proposed to improve or even to change radically the traditional methods of planning and managing the national economy. The overall aim of all those proposed changes, both in theory and in practice, is to improve economic efficiency, by making the communist economic system more rational and better suited to the needs of a modern industrial society. The main instrument required to achieve these objectives has been defined by Poland's Professor Brus as a "regulated market mechanism" (143). "Regulated," of course, by central planners. This means in essence that the state retains the monopoly of all policy decisions on the macro-economic scale, while gradually increasing the freedom of action of lower echelons at the micro-economic level.

This spontaneous outbreak of economic revisionism has not, as yet, produced a new comprehensive theory of running the national economy, or evolved an alternative system of planning and management. Both the critical analyses and the concrete reformist measures proposed so far, have been confined to partial solutions of specific problems and do not yet add up to a coherent whole (156). Nevertheless, a common pattern of all those reform proposals is already emerging. Despite inevitable differences of approach, of emphasis, and of objective economic conditions, the general aim of all the reform blueprints is: a) to better equate the actual output with effective demand, b) to replace growth promotion through new investments by higher productivity of the existing productive potential and c) to harness individual initiative so as to achieve in a more effective way the ultimate economic objectives set forth by central planners—in short, to run the socialized economy in a more rational way (143).

Before one examines the scope and direction of this revisionist thinking as it has appeared in the various countries of the Soviet bloc, a few other general points have to be established. Economic revisionism represents the second stage of destalinization. The first stage, as we have seen it in the various countries of the bloc, has been largely political and its effects largely confined to the party. However important the concessions made to the population, the essential result of the first stage of destalinization has been a sort of personal charter of security for the holder of a party card. The reestablishment of party supremacy over the secret police required the end of terror. The concessions granted to the population at large were incidental to this basic process of curbing the powers of the secret police. In the course of this process, the individual parties had to purge themselves of the most compromised members of their hierarchies and rehabilitate victims of the s sonality cult.

But experience has shown that the purges and the reh (of which again the party members were the principal aries), and the important concessions granted to the po have not in any way undermined the basis of the commun tem. Apparently this system can survive some degree of libe tion, as long as the concessions granted do not infringe on the basis of its power: the dictatorship of the party.

The second phase of destalinization, economic revisionism, is in a sense more important than the first because it strikes at the economic roots of the party's power. The very essence of the prevailing trend in economic thinking, as we shall see, is the transfer of decision-making power, at least in the field of micro-economics, from party leaders to the new managerial class and eventually, through the mechanism of the market, to the population as a whole. Moreover, the accompanying changes in the economic thinking of the communist elite and also in the methods of planning and running the national economies would seriously weaken the ideological basis of orthodox communism. Economic revisionism must inevitably lead to political pragmatism, since in a Marxist system politics and economics are inseparably linked together. As a Czech writer has put it:

> The proposals for a new system of management have been based on criticism of the administrative-directive centralism, not on the rejection of the extensive method of economy alone. A connection between economics and politics is absolutely clear in this respect and our present efforts cannot be limited to questions of economic management but must aim at the creation of general conditions for a more democratic administration and of a rational political system with strictly defined powers. (20)[3]

The same thesis has been expressed even more forcefully by the prominent Hungarian Marxist philosopher, György Lukacs. In an exclusive interview, published in the Italian communist party organ *L'Unita,* he described the economic reforms as a much needed and sought after opportunity for the democratization of the basic political institutions of the communist society (135).

---

[3] The same idea is also discussed at much greater length by I. Bistrina (18).

According to Lukacs, a new economic model is the first essential step toward correction the effects of "dogmatic and sectarian backwardness," which accumulated during the Stalin era. Lukacs claimed that economic reforms can only succeed in an atmosphere of "proletarian democracy," which he defined as "democratic co-operation between Party leadership and the masses aimed at a relentless and decisive elimination of bureaucracy."

Another reason why economic revisionism is a logical second stage in the process of destalinization is that the regime of terror was an essential factor in the stalinist economic system. It enabled the authorities to impose excessive forced savings on all strata of the population.[4] It enabled them to bleed agriculture white for the sake of capital accumulation in industry. It kept the workers quiet in the face of unprecedented exploitation. It provided man-power, forced labor if necessary, wherever it was needed. Finally, it kept the managerial class in check. When the use of police methods had to be abandoned, the need arose for a new system of incentives.

The end of terror and force also enabled the economists to speak more freely. No doubt, even in the forties and the early fifties many Soviet bloc economists were fully aware of the inadequacy of the existing economic system. However, the fate of the Soviet Chairman of the State Planning Committee (Gosplan), N. A. Voznesensky, hardly encouraged them to express their ideas openly and much less to put forward concrete reform proposals.[5] Only after the relaxation of secret police terror in the mid nineteen-fifties was there an outbreak of intellectual ferment, which embraced all fields of scientific, literary, and artistic activity.

It is by no means a coincidence that this intellectual ferment

---

[4] Forced savings in the form of artificially low wages, compulsory delivery prices for agricultural produce, and forced subscription of state loans were the main source of capital accumulation in the Stalin era.

[5] The reasons for the downfall and subsequent liquidation of Voznesensky have not yet been fully clarified, but there is ample evidence that, besides the standard conflict of personalities involved in a power struggle, at least one of the reasons for purging him was his attempt to effect a complete overhaul of the Soviet wholesale price system. His price reform went into effect on January 1, 1949. The apparent intention was to establish a more rational relationship between factory prices and profit. After the downfall of Voznesensky, his price reform was revised (226).

had its most lasting effect in the field of economics. One can always produce dialectical reasons for reimposing party control in the fields of art and literature. Besides, the issue of artistic freedom is of less immediate interest to people in general than economic questions, which are bread and butter issues.

One has to bear in mind that economic revisionism arises not only from the intellectual ferment among economists and from the growing frustration of the managerial class, but even more from the growing popular pressure for a higher standard of living (46). The party leaders are fully aware of the wastefulness and the irrationality of the existing economic system, even though they have always acclaimed it as the ultimate achievement in scientific rationality and efficiency. The evidence on every hand cannot be ignored. This is why even the most dogmatic party leaders pay some lip service to the need for far-reaching economic reforms. It is politically impossible to stop the publication of ever more revisionistic theses, particularly since their avowed aim is only to make the system better, to stop the discussion, and to prevent more far-reaching reforms. The party leaders and other dogmatic elements can only fight a rearguard action employing procrastination, delaying tactics, misrepresentation of the proposed reforms, and the general inertia of the system, assisted by those who have vested interests in maintaining the status quo.

This type of resistance has indeed been evident in every Soviet bloc country, where economic reforms were carried beyond the stage of purely theoretical discussions. The existence of such an opposition has been publicly acknowledged by Czechoslovak Premier Lenart in his speech at the 13th Party Congress in Prague,[6] (65) by Professor Evsei Liberman in a statement published by the Italian Communist Party weekly *Rinascita*,[7] and by Professor Ota Sik in an interview with the Slovak trade union daily *Praca* (50). As Professor Sik put it, "Some people are backing the new system with words, but in practice they do everything to retain the old ways." The various forms of this obstinate rearguard action, which

---

[6] The text of this speech was published in *Rude Pravo* (June 3, 1966).

[7] "*La Riforma non e un'eresia*" (the reform is no heresy), a round table discussion between Profs. Evsei Liberman, Sylos Labini (University of Rome), and Sign. Napolitano (Italian communist party), (December 31, 1966), 13–14.

succeeded in slowing down and diluting economic reforms almost everywhere, will be discussed in more detail in the appropriate chapters of this book.

The first systematic attack upon the orthodox methods of economic planning and industrial management was carried out in Yugoslavia in the early fifties. But the Yugoslav communists had by then already been expelled from the world communist movement and condemned as heretics. Their leaders were working feverishly to forge closer political and economic bonds with the population, their only hope of survival if they were not to rely totally on the West. Thus, the early reforms in Yugoslavia were carried out from above, by the party leadership acting in exceptional political circumstances. For this reason Yugoslav economic revisionism must be treated as a different phenomenon from that now appearing in the Soviet bloc.

The fact remains that the Yugoslav experiment, as it gradually evolved, has had a great influence on economic thinking in the Soviet bloc, especially in Bulgaria (3). Its main importance, however, lies in that it offers a ready-made alternative to the traditional communist economic system. Much of the really revisionist economic thinking within the Soviet bloc goes far beyond the bounds of the Yugoslav experiment, while sharing with it the main trend of development: a clear desire to revert to a market economy. (19).

The political rapprochement between the Soviet bloc and Yugoslavia in recent years has made the Yugoslav experiment a legitimate subject of study and scientific appraisal. The very fact that a working alternative exists for the traditional system doubtless gives a powerful stimulus to intellectual ferment in economic theory and practice.

But all this does not detract from the importance of quite a different factor, namely the tremendous impact made by the unprecedented prosperity of Western Europe. The communist bloc is today no longer a tightly isolated, closed society; it was in Stalin's time. Since 1956, first the Poles and later the Hungarians, the Czechs and even many Russians were able to travel relatively freely to the West. The East Germans of course have the standard of comparison at their own doorstep. The West European prosperity soon became a legend throughout the communist bloc. The fact that the system of free market economy could secure such a rapid growth rate, while at the same time ensuring general affluence, has made a powerful impression on the people who live under communist rule. Since the prosperity in the West happened to coincide with the growing economic difficulties in the communist bloc, it became the source of acute embarrassment to all the apologists of the traditional Marxist-Leninist economic system. There is ample evidence of the impact made by Western prosperity, in the form of dozens of press articles, trying desperately to explain away the embarrassing contrast of the "capitalist" affluence with the grim reality throughout the communist bloc.[8] This also helped to create a situation in which pragmatic economic thinking became inevitable.

The impact of the Western prosperity on economic thinking in the Soviet bloc can be seen in various attempts to incorporate the principles of a market economy into the framework of central planning. In Poland at least a score of books have been written on the subject, the most serious and comprehensive by Professor Brus (199). Another consequence has been the resurrection of such "bourgeois" concepts as economic self-interest, material incentives, interest on capital, and even profitability.

In essence this meant a rehabilitation of hedonistic behavior and the profit motive. Profit, once the very symbol of avaricious and corrupt capitalism, is now being recommended as "the best measuring rod to assess the economic efficiency of any socialized enterprise" (120). And yet not so long ago the very word "profit" was still like the proverbial red rag to a bull for any Marxist believer. Profit, or rather the profit motive, was made into a symbol of all the alleged exploitative and usurious characteristics of the "capitalist" system. Ignoring the conclusions of any objective economic analysis, Soviet bloc economists persisted in equating profits with the so-called "surplus value."[9] Today the situation has changed considerably. In an attempt to inject some degree of

---

[8] For instance, "In a Great Measure We Are Catching Up with the Level of Living Standards in the West" *Rude Pravo* (November 22, 1966). "Trouble with a Picture" *Kultura* (November 20, 1966); J. Zielinski (176); H. Flakierski (150).

[9] Even after the new economic model was proposed in Poland, the Economic Dictionary (pub. State Economic Publications [PWE] Warsaw, 1958), insisted on equating "profit" with "surplus value" (pp. 936–37).

rationality into their own economic system, the communist planners are now prepared to recognize profit as the "best synthetic indicator of all economic activity" (155). This, of course, is closely connected with the general tendency toward the establishment of the principle of profitability as the basis for evolving a system of planning and industrial management in which economic incentives would replace arbitrary directives, at least at the microeconomic level (200, pp. 54–69).

What does such an ideological rehabilitation of profit mean in practical terms? Ostensibly, the whole issue is concerned with nothing more than the theory of economic planning and the technique of management. The proposed changes would consist of replacing the hitherto basic indicator, that is the value of global production, by the synthetic concept of profit (200, pp. 56–57). Such a substitution is supposed to provide a magic cure for all the main defects of the communist economic system. But will it? And are we really dealing here only with the methods of planning and the technique of management?

Let us reflect for a while on what are the likely long-term effects of replacing the indicator of global production with that of profit. One could well claim that in the long run the adoption of the concept of profit must lead to a fundamental change, as far as the real objectives of all economic activity are concerned. For what were the practical effects of the preponderance of the indicator of global production? In their essence they boiled down to the fact that all efforts were directed toward achieving the highest possible value of the annual output (142). This was, after all, the basic criterion for assessing the performance of any socialized enterprise, irrespective of whether the structure of this output was related to market requirements.

The main drawback of this system was the ever-growing disparity between actual production and effective demand. The managers of individual factories had but one aim: to produce as many goods as possible, regardless of the actual cost of production and, worse still, regardless of whether there was any effective demand for those goods.

It is, of course, difficult to believe that the introduction of the principle of profitability could change from one day to another the psychological attitude of the managers of socialized enterprises. But, in the long run, such change is unavoidable. For the concept of profit encompasses not only actual production of goods, but also their effective sale (48). Such an interpretation of the meaning of profit—and there cannot be any other one—introduces a direct connection between output and effective demand. In other words, a producer who is guided by the profit motive must pay close attention to the needs of the market (165).

In this way, at least as far as consumer goods are concerned, the rehabilitation of the concept of profit must eventually lead to the next logical step: a tacit acceptance of the principle of the sovereignty of the consumer. And from here it is not very far to the adoption of all the essential vestiges of market economy. This is confirmed by the tendencies evident in the rapid change-over of the Yugoslav economic system in the last year or two[10] and by certain trends discernible in the Polish, Czechoslovak, Hungarian, and East German reforms.

But one must have no illusions that the mere acceptance of the principle of profitability will, by itself, logically lead to the return of market economy. The problem here is not only one of the unavoidable resistance of dogmatic elements, but also a more important question of objective difficulties.[11] Besides, the profit motive cannot work effectively within the framework of a system of arbitrarily determined wages and prices, which the party leaders are obviously unwilling to give up.

And here let us reflect for a moment on the true meaning of profit. From the purely bookkeeping point of view, profit is merely the difference between the cost of production and the selling price. Now, under the existing communist economic system, the central planners still retain the power to dictate the prices of raw materials, of semi-finished products, and of fuel and power, as well as the upper limit of the so-called "wage funds." Thus, within a certain margin determined by efficiency, the central planners exert major influence on the costs of production of any enterprise. At the same time those central planners more often than not fix the selling

---

[10] That is, since the second stage of economic reform was put into effect in July 1965.

[11] These objective difficulties are discussed at length in Chapter 4 of this book.

price.[12] This means that (again within a certain margin) they can effectively determine the size of profits. Worse still, the planners can still manipulate these profits at will, either by raising or lowering either the production costs (through their components), or by changing the selling price.

What conclusions can be drawn from all this? The acceptance of profit as the main indicator of all economic activity is, no doubt, a step in the right direction. But this rational measure cannot remedy the main shortcomings of the communist economic system, until the practice of arbitrary price and wage fixing is abandoned. But this means giving up what the older generation of party leaders and Marxist theoreticians still regard as the "essence of socialist planning" (193).

Any significant break with the residual vestiges of economic centralism can be made only by the new generation of economists and technocrats (which already includes some influential party members). These people are not only better educated, but also more rational in their approach to the economic problems than the old cadres of party leaders. This new generation is much more inclined to reject outdated theoretical dogmas in favor of pragmatic solutions. It feels increasingly frustrated, both by the ineffectiveness of the old system and by the thwarting of its own managerial ambitions. In the long run, this young elite can be expected to generate enough pressure to force through the necessary reforms both in economic theory and in methods of planning and managing the national economy. But their pressure can become politically effective only if it receives the support of the broad masses of the population.

---

[12] See Chapter 4 for a more detailed discussion of the prevailing price determination practices.

2

★

POLAND: THE FRUSTRATED PIONEER

The rapid spread of economic revisionism throughout the Soviet bloc was the compound effect of the interplay of various political, social, and economic factors. Some of those factors have been negative: persistent economic difficulties, the frustration of the managerial class and the intellectual elite, and the growing realization of the inadequacy of the economic system inherited from the stalinist era and its accompanying institutions. Others have been positive: the liberalization of the intellectual climate, the end of the system of terror, the Yugoslav experiment, and the overall impact of the prosperity attained in Western Europe under a free-market economy.

One may now pass on to a brief outline of the main trends in revisionist economic thinking as they have manifested themselves in various countries of the Soviet bloc. Since economic revisionism is really the second stage of the process of destalinization, one should not be surprised to find its manifestations occurring after the beginning of the stage of political relaxation and intellectual liberalization. The only exception to this rule is East Germany, where Ulbricht is trying to emulate Tito's earlier example and impose some elements of a market-oriented economic system from above, without a prior relaxation in the political and cultural fields.[1] But elsewhere economic revisionism developed after at least a brief period of political destalinization.

---

[1] The first blueprint for economic reforms in East Germany (90) was published at the height of a periodic turning of political screws.

This being so, one should not be surprised that the first real attempt to introduce meaningful economic reforms occurred in Poland, the first Soviet bloc country to experience a major upsurge of political liberalization, after its bloodless revolution of October 1956. At that time, the economic pragmatism in Poland enjoyed the apparent (if not very sincere) official backing of the new party leadership. Indeed, the green light for economic reforms was given by Gomulka himself as soon as he was elected the new First Secretary of the Polish Communist Party (PUWP.) (185, pp. 30–34). Soon afterward, in response to popular pressure for a basic change in the existing economic system of centralized planning, the Gomulka regime called into being the Economic Council, a special body composed of some of the most prominent Polish economists. The main task of this council was to prepare the blueprint for a new Polish economic model (177). During 1957, the Economic Council elaborated and published two basic documents, which contained both the theoretical premises of the new model as well as concrete proposals for the necessary reforms.[2] These two official documents were supplemented by dozens of articles published by the chief protagonists of the "Polish economic model." Together they provided a definite blueprint of a completely new system of planning and management, perhaps the most comprehensive program of economic reform produced up to date anywhere in the Soviet bloc. At the same time the Gomulka regime began putting into effect its "new agrarian policy," based on a return to private farming and gradual reintroduction of market relations in agriculture.[3]

Let us now analyze the proposals of the Economic Council in more detail. The Polish blueprint called for two kinds of basic changes in the economic system. One was a drastic reorganization of the administration and management of the economy, emphasizing decentralization and the financial independence of individual enterprises (163). The second category of proposed reforms sought to inject quasi-market conditions into the relations between state enterprises and wholesale and retail distribution. The basic

---

2 This blueprint consisted of two basic documents (187, 188).

3 The basic features of this new agrarian policy are extensively discussed in Chapter 9 of this book.

overall aim was to substitute "the profit motive and other economic incentives for administrative directives as the mainspring of economic activity" (142).

On the side of reorganization, the Polish blueprint called for dismantling the bureaucratic superstructure of the economy. The basic economic unit was to be the self-governing and fully independent enterprise (162). Each of these independent economic units was to operate according to the principles of cost accounting and the highest possible degree of profitability was to be the main concern of its director (acting together with the workers' council, which had at that time full rights of co-management). The self-governing enterprise was to sell its products to other factories and to the distributive enterprises at prices "which would be primarily determined by the real costs of production and the forces of the market mechanism" (168). All forms of state-subsidized production were to be discontinued.

To bring about quasi-market conditions, in which the profit motive could function as the mainspring of economic activity, the Economic Council theses provided for a general reform of wages and prices. The aim was to bring the prices of raw materials, semi-finished products, and finished articles in line with the real cost of production. To compensate the population for the expected increase in the level of prices and consequently in the cost of living, there was to be a substantial increase in wages and other sources of income (188). The Economic Council maintained that once the proper relationship between prices, production costs, and incomes had been established, then normal economic incentives, acting within the framework of a market mechanism, would provide the motive force for all future economic activity. The output of any given commodity would be determined by its price and the demand for it. At the same time, competition would keep prices down (140).

Two things must be obvious even from this brief outline of the Polish economic model: first, the strong influence of the Yugoslav experiment on the economic thinking of the main protagonists of the reforms.[4] Second, that the Economic Council's proposals went

[4] This is evidenced by the large number of analytical studies of the Yugoslav system, which were published in Polish economic periodicals in early 1957.

far beyond the Yugoslav system as it was at that time, and amounted to the substitution of the principles of market economy (with some vestiges of centralized planning) for the traditional communist economic system (159).

The main mistake of Polish economic revisionism in the 1956–57 period was that its protagonists wanted to achieve too much. The time was not yet ripe for this kind of thinking in the Soviet bloc. Indeed a strong pressure was then put on the Gomulka regime to stop playing with fire. This is now admitted quite openly. Professor Brus, one of the original members of the Economic Council and one of the chief protagonists of the Polish economic model, reviewed the progress of economic reforms throughout the bloc at the end of 1966. While underlining the similarities of various reform blueprints, he made the following rueful remark:

> The rather large degree of similarity in the reforms now being implemented in various socialist countries is particularly worthy of emphasis, since the reforms have been arrived at only in recent years. *Ten years ago, when basically analogical changes were promoted in a particularly advanced fashion in Poland, the attitudes were sharply different and in the majority of the socialist countries, strongly critical evaluation was clearly in evidence.* (143, p. 11) [italics added]

This hostile outside pressure was only one of the factors which precluded the practical implementation of the Polish economic model. The fact that fundamental changes in the existing economic system were worked out in Poland so much in advance of the rest of the bloc and that revisionist economic concepts were openly propagated even in official party organs, can be explained only by the weakness of the party apparatus following the events of October 1956. But a reaction soon set in. By the middle of 1958 the traditionalist elements in the party leadership had regained the initiative and were able to frustrate all attempts to implement the reforms advocated by the Economic Council (and approved in principle by the Polish government).[5] Although some structural

Brus wrote a series of five articles under the common title, "A Closer Look at the Yugoslav System" (146), and R. Fidelski published an article on "System of Industrial Management in Yugoslavia" (149).

5 Stefan Jedrychowski, Poland's Chief Planner, declared in an interview in

changes foreseen in the blueprint were carried out, they were vitiated by the survival of the bureaucratic superstructure and by the system of administrative directives. Many experiments intended as pilot schemes for the New Economic Model were deliberately sabotaged and obstructed by dogmatic elements in the party leadership. The proposed reform of wages and prices was abandoned altogether.[6]

But while the practical implementation of the Polish economic model was effectively frustrated by the party leadership, its basic theoretical concepts were kept alive and even further developed during 1948–63. True, the main protagonists of the Polish economic model were removed from positions where they could influence the actual economic policy.[7] But unable any longer to propagate their ideas in the dailies and periodicals, the Polish pragmatists began to study the problems of economic reforms in depth. During the blackest period of centralist restoration, a substantial number of highly sophisticated books and scientific publications, dealing with various theoretical aspects of the proposed reforms, were published in Poland (see 199–204).

The return to a centralized economic system and the methods of direct controls[8] inevitably brought about serious economic difficulties, which reached their climax in the winter of 1962–63. Consequently, in the fall of 1963 the Polish party leaders again began to look more critically at their economic machinery, and a Central Committee plenum in November examined the errors that had been committed in planning and management (see 189). This led to renewed interest in the reforms that had been advocated in earlier years. In March 1964 the party, preparing for its Fourth Congress

---

Trybuna Ludu (November 21, 1957), that the proposals of the Economic Council pertaining to structural and organizational changes in industry were "accepted in principle by the [Polish] government."

6 Unlike the structural changes, the proposed reform of the system of wages and prices was never accepted by the powers that be. The theses on determination of principles of price structure were only published in *Zycie Gospodarcze* but never in the party press. It seems that the very notion of a market price was not acceptable to party leadership.

7 The Economic Council became moribund by 1959 and was finally dissolved at the end of 1962.

8 Early in 1960 the competences of central planners were greatly strengthened (see 138).

in June, published a set of theses outlining its basic economic program. The theses contained a chapter on "Methods of Planning and Management," in which the party leadership set forth some of the revisionist thinking of its own (190, pp. 111–15).

Thus, after an interval of nearly six years, economic pragmatism again became a part of the official policy line in Poland. But the situation was not quite the same as in early post-October 1956. At that time, the dogmatic elements in the Polish party had been decisively routed and were in full political retreat. The liberal wing and the economic pragmatists had an upper hand. By 1963 the political balance within the party leadership had been completely reversed and the influence of the hardliners was again predominant.

This political situation has a direct bearing on the spirit in which the new dose of economic reforms is being implemented in Poland. The Polish economic model of 1956–57 reflected the pragmatic thinking of the then-leading personalities among Gomulka's close associates.[9] In the mid-sixties the leadership of the PUWP considers rational reforms of the economic system a necessary evil, which they are forced to introduce against their natural dogmatic instinct and almost against their better judgment. The protagonists of the Polish economic model of 1956–57 were genuinely convinced that the traditional, centralist system of planning and managing the national economy had outlived any usefulness it ever had. The present leadership of the Polish party distrusts and fears any changes, which must inevitably weaken their firm hold on the economy. If they do support certain reforms, it is because they see no other alternative. The state of Polish economy is so precarious and has deteriorated so much in the last few years that the leadership of the PUWP is willing to try out any remedy, even if it instinctively distrusts the prescription. But they do it half-heartedly and are constantly hedging every small step toward necessary reforms with a new dose of bureaucratic control.

This lack of political will to proceed along the road of pragmatism explains the different approach to economic reforms in the

---

[9] Among them, the late Professor Oscar Lange, then Chairman of the Economic Council, and Central Committee Secretaries J. Morawski and W. Matwin. Morawski was removed in October 1959 and Matwin in December 1963.

middle sixties. After October 1956, Poland jumped head first into the then virtually uncharted seas of economic revisionism. Today, she cautiously dips her toe in. But the external situation has also changed considerably. When the principles of the Polish economic model were being formulated, Poland was the only country within the Soviet bloc (Yugoslavia was very much outside at that time) which intended to break away from the system of directive planning and bureaucratic control. The main argument of the opponents of the Polish Model was that its implementation would create a "basic disproportion" between the Polish economic system and that of the other communist countries.[10] Besides, the attitude of the Soviet Union and other East European countries to the reforms proposed in Poland was openly critical, if not well-nigh hostile.

By 1964 the situation was changed. A wave of economic pragmatism has transformed what has been a purely Polish effort into a general bloc-wide trend.[11] The "disproportion" argument was no longer valid and controlled economic revisionism had become respectable, both ideologically and politically. Thus, while the internal political atmosphere was certainly less favorable from the point of view of the protagonists of pragmatic reforms, the external situation within the bloc was infinitely better.

This fact strengthened the hand of the protagonists of a more rational economic system, both within the PUWP hierarchy and among Poland's top economists and intellectuals. They cleverly reversed the disproportion argument, used against them in the period after October 1956, by pointing out that Poland, which pioneered the drive for a new economic model in the mid-fifties, is now being left behind.

Typical of this type of argument was the speech made late in 1964 in the Polish Parliament (Sejm) by Konstanty Lubienski, a deputy belonging to the Catholic group, Znak:[12]

---

[10] This type of argument was advanced publicly by such extreme hardliners as W. Klosiewicz and St. Lapot at the 11th Plenum of the Polish CC (February 27–March 1, 1958). Cf. *New York Times,* March 2, 1958 and *Neue Zuercher Zeitung,* March 3, 1958.

[11] See Chapter 3 of this book for more detailed description of the development of pragmatic thinking and practices in the rest of the bloc during 1963–64.

[12] The Znak group is a purely Polish political phenomenon. It is an association of non-communist leftish Catholic intellectuals, which is allowed to publish

The reform of the system of planning and managing the national economy has become the central issue in all the socialist countries, and, therefore, the Sejm of the Polish People's Republic is not in a position to ignore this subject. It would appear, however, that the rate at which such changes are being introduced in Poland is excessively slow, and the directions of the changes are not always the right ones.

As is well known, Poland was the first socialist country to become interested in this matter, in the years 1956–58, and probably made an important contribution to the search for the right solutions. One needs only to recall the lively discussion which was carried out in those years, as well as the Theses of the Economic Council outlining the basic directions of the changes. It should be stressed that those Theses were the work of our most outstanding economists. . . . No wonder that they became an object of interest to the other socialist countries.

But today one gets the impression that our neighbors are getting ahead of us, not only in the boldness of the problems which they decided to tackle, but also in terms of the speed with which they are introducing the necessary reforms in practice. . . . The First Secretary of the CC of the PUWP was quite right when he said that nobody can know more than the enterprise concerned about the hidden economic reserves and about the best methods for their utilization. The conclusion is simple: One has to create such a system of administration and planning that would permit our enterprises to find these reserves and make the best use out of them. But in order to achieve this, it is necessary to change radically our entire system of planning and managing the national economy.[13]

Deputy Lubienski can by no means be regarded as the most outstanding or the most authoritative protagonist of economic reforms in Poland. But, being a member of parliament, he was able to say publicly and openly, what the better-known and much more competent advocates of economic pragmatism were saying either in more esoteric press articles or behind the closed doors of communist party caucuses (see 160, 166, 169, 170). There is no doubt,

---

its own weekly (*Tygodnik Powszechny*) and to present a limited number of candidates at the parliamentary elections. Unlike the notorious PAX group, it does not openly collaborate with the regime but acts as a sort of "loyal opposition."

[13] This is the censored text of the Lubienski speech in *Tygodnik Powszechny* (January 3, 1965). Incidentally, Mr. Lubienski's candidature was not approved by the party authorities in the next parliamentary elections in May 1965.

however, that ever since the economic troubles of 1962–63, the leadership of the PUWP was being subjected to a constant and growing pressure for speeding up the pace of economic reforms, a pressure coming both from without the party hierarchy and from within.

This constant prodding, under the battle cry "too little and too slow," has been carried out in the face of a deliberate rear-guard action of the dogmatic elements. The main tactics of the dogmatic establishment have been to pay lip service to the need for economic reform, while putting it off as long as possible and then watering down the actual implementation. This means that each accepted reformist measure is being neutralized by injecting it with a stiff dose of bureaucratic and administrative control.[14]

This has happened even with the party's own pre-Congress theses. The reformist postulates outlined therein were watered down considerably during the editorial work on the final text of the resolution of the IV Party Congress. Nevertheless, Chapter XIV of this resolution entitled "Methods of Planning and Management" did contain some residue of pragmatic economic thinking so vehemently expressed in pre-Congress theses. The resolution stated clearly that "profit should be henceforth accepted as the main measuring rod of economic efficiency" and that "profitability of production and strict cost accounting should be the basic criteria of all economic activity" (191). The party Congress also gave its approval to the principle that every decision to produce a given line of goods must be preceded by adequate market research. Finally, the Congress resolution acknowledged the need for a greater degree of decentralization of economic decision making.

All this could well give the impression that the progress along the road of economic rationalism has been resumed, although at a slower pace. However, the actual situation in Poland (and elsewhere in the bloc as well) is full of inherent contradictions and potential pitfalls. By stressing unduly the texts of the proposed reforms and their overall trend, one may create an impression of a smooth progress of economic reforms, an impression which would be quite misleading. On the other hand, an undue emphasis on the

---

[14] This point is amply documented in the description of some post-IV Congress reform measures outlined in the concluding part of this chapter.

hedging tactics of the party leadership, which tend to perpetuate the system of direct controls, may give an equally inaccurate picture of complete stagnation. The truth, as usual, lies somewhere in between those two extremes. While the rear-guard action of the dogmatic elements has no doubt succeeded to the extent of slowing down the implementation of pragmatic solutions and of rendering the accepted reforms less effective, the situation is by no means static. Besides, one should make a clear distinction between the short-term effects of the dogmatic countermeasures and the long-term dynamics of the reforms themselves.

It is quite true to say that in Poland, as elsewhere in the bloc, the drive to rationalize and reform the existing economic system has hardly got beyond the stage of certain practical measures and of proclaiming a set of rather general principles. But, in any economy, the acceptance of the theoretical premises of the overall policy is the indispensable first step toward gradually evolving suitable practical solutions. Once those principles are generally and unequivocally accepted, one may presume that the proper institutional changes will follow in due course.

This optimistic presumption may seem inconsistent with the actual practice of hedging the proposed reforms with countermeasures, which obviously aim at perpetuating the system of centralized, direct controls and arbitrary decision-making. Why should the dogmatist elements within the party hierarchy accept pragmatic principles, while at the same time insist on safeguards which are bound to render the proposed practical solutions, based on those principles, inoperative. This is not always a case of conscious sabotage. The main reason for the apparent inconsistency is that the same abstract concepts do not mean the same thing to the dogmatists within the party hierarchy as to the more pragmatic economists, party intellectuals, and technocrats. *Mutatis mutandis*—it is the same type of terminological confusion as when Stalin, Churchill, and Roosevelt agreed in Yalta that there should be "free elections" in Poland. The fact is that the terms "economic effectiveness," "profitability," or "optimal production" have a completely different meaning for the members of the ruling party establishment than for people like professor Oscar Lange, or other protagonists of pragmatic reforms. Thus, the two sides can agree on a set of abstract principles, or even a text of a concrete reform proposal (as Stalin, Churchill, and Roosevelt did in the text of the Yalta communiqué), but they must inevitably fall apart at the stage of practical implementation. This is because the basic aim of the party establishment is to introduce a greater degree of efficiency and rationality into the existing economic system, while retaining full-scale control (which would still permit them to determine the order of economic priorities and allocation of economic resources). The genuine protagonists of economic reform have, on the other hand, a different ultimate objective. They want to change the system itself, so that it would eventually operate on the basis of purely objective economic considerations.

This contradiction in ultimate aims is by no means a specifically Polish phenomenon. The same situation exists in every country of the Moscow bloc. Everywhere the old-timers and dogmatists are yielding to a strong pressure which forces them to introduce the necessary reforms, while at the same time doing their best to slow down the progress and retain a decisive degree of control. The real point is that what is needed for effective economic reform is not only a set of general principles and attractively designed reform blueprints, but first of all, a subjective political will of the people in authority to carry out that reform in good faith and to accept its full logical implications. This political will is still absent among the party old guard, not only in Poland but also elsewhere in the bloc. In contrast, the younger generation even among the party hierarchy has a completely different approach to those problems. And for this reason, while bearing in mind the short-term effects of the rearguard actions of the old-timers, one can be more optimistic about the long-term prospects of economic reform.

This rather lengthy aside is necessary to put the reforms introduced in Poland in the mid-sixties in their proper perspective. But it has also a more general validity. In essence, the political atmosphere, in which economic reforms are being introduced, is quite similar throughout the whole bloc. Bearing this general political situation in mind, the reader may perhaps better understand the apparent inconsistencies between the individual reform proposals, as described in Chapter 3 of this book, and some general aspects of practical implementation discussed in the following chapters. The essential fact to remember is that not only in Poland, but in all other Soviet bloc countries as well (and in Yugoslavia too for that matter) all economic reforms are an outcome of an intense political struggle in which the dogmatic old guard temporarily still has an upper hand. Hence, the short-term effects are likely to be limited. On the other hand, the overall trend of all those reforms is in the direction of an ever-growing degree of pragmatism. Thus there is some progress. It may be slow, hesitant, sometimes even frustrating—but a progress which no one can deny.

One example of this type of progress is the fragmentary reforms introduced in Poland in the mid-sixties. Some four weeks after the IV Congress, the Polish government promulgated a lengthy decree which was meant to provide a partial institutional framework for practical measures necessary to implement decisions of the Congress(192). In fact, however, the decree of July 29, 1964 was in part an organizational blueprint and in part yet another declaration of principles.

On the practical side, the text of the decree provided for some significant institutional changes, the gist of them being that certain new posts in the industrial hierarchy were to be reserved for individuals with recognized economic qualifications. Also several advisory bodies, staffed by professional economists and statisticians, were to be created at all levels of industrial structure from the ministry down to individual enterprises (192, pp. 4–6). The main purpose of all these institutional changes was to ensure that the set of principles, elaborated upon elsewhere in the text of the decree, was adhered to in all economic decision-making concerning the actual output of industry.

The first of these principles was one of "economic effectiveness, based on a strict cost accounting." This meant, as explained in the decree, that all production plans must be justified by purely economic considerations, such as the existence of unsatisfied demand or the estimated profitability of the proposed output. The second principle was overall profitability of any enterprise. This in turn meant that every industrial undertaking had a right to use its resources in such a way as to make the maximum profit. Finally, the third principle insisted on adapting the production plans to effective demand. The decree stated clearly that each industrial undertaking must conduct a detailed market analysis to ascertain the potential demand for the products it intended to manufacture and base its production plans on the results of such surveys.

The decree was certainly an important document. But being obviously a compromise between the opposing trends in the PUWP leadership, its text was often contradictory, confusing, and unnecessarily verbose.[15] Like every document of this type, it contains both positive and negative features. This is inevitable since the party authorities attempted to achieve the impossible: to reconcile certain elements of economic pragmatism and decentralization of decision-making with the traditional bureaucratic superstructure of the communist system and its time-honored prerogatives of control. The result is that the various provisions of the decree create a fertile ground for fomenting contradictory trends in all sectors of the national economy.

The positive aspect can be seen in the acceptance of market analysis as the obligatory basis for determination of output structure, and of strict cost accounting as the sole objective criterion of all economic decision-making. In this sense, the Polish decree may, in the long run, bring about the end of a *dirigiste* type of economy, which prevailed in Poland for more than twenty years. As already indicated, the decree makes it obligatory for the central economic institutions, the ministries, the industrial associations (trusts), and the individual enterprises to base their overall planning and production schedules on the principles of economic effectiveness, strict cost accounting, and market analysis. Besides, the decree introduces one more essential change from the traditional practices of communist planning. Instead of a single and authoritative national plan, both the industrial associations and the individual enterprises will receive several variants of the draft plan. And the final choice of the actual version of the plan to be adopted is to be based on the results of an objective economic analysis.

So far, so good. Unfortunately however, the text of the decree is also replete with bureaucratic safeguards which tend to neutralize the positive aspects of it. It is enough to say that all economic activity necessary to implement the new system is to be directed, coordinated, and controlled by not less than ten central institutions, not counting the ministries concerned. From the Planning Commission, through the Committee on Science and Technology

---

[15] The text of the decree occupies more than eleven pages of *Monitor Polski.*

and the Committee on Labor and Wages, to the State Commission on Prices, each of these ten central institutions is to have its say in the making of the more essential decisions (192, pp. 9–10).

At the same time, the text of the decree provides no answer to the most crucial question: What should be done in the case of a clear conflict between a production plan based on objective, economic premises and a course of action dictated by political or ideological considerations? This is in no way an abstract possibility. Under the communist system one has to reckon all the time with directives of the party authorities which tend to allocate economic resources to some projects, which is obviously not the most rational way of using the available economic means. What would happen if such a conflict between the economic analysis and ideology did arise? What should be done in the case where objective cost accounting would show that a decision made by party leadership is uneconomic and irrational? Which would then prevail: the principle of economic effectiveness or political expediency?

The crucial issue here is the extent to which objective economic premises would be permitted to play a decisive role in the process of productive decision-making. The system of planning and management, outlined in the decree, clearly envisages that comparative economic cost accounting and market analysis should form the basis of all production plans. But such purely economic considerations, as well as the preferences of the consumers, reflected in the results of market research analysis, may well run counter to the established political and ideological priorities. And hence, there is not only a possibility but a probability of a conflict arising between an objective evaluation based on rational economic premises, and the directives of the central authorities which spring from doctrinaire ideological considerations.

In the short run, at least, such conflicts—when they do arise—are likely to be resolved in favor of doctrinal priorities. The text of the Polish decree contains definite stipulations which make it abundantly clear that the party authorities still retain the prerogative of making ultimate decisions. For this reason, the pragmatic reforms which this decree purports to foster must be considered as only half measures. One would expect that the pragmatic principles would prove more operative in respect to consumer goods production where the alternative use of resources would not, as a rule, involve doctrinal considerations. But where the choice is between more rational use of economic resources, as indicated in market requirements and the dictates of Marxist dogmas, the doctrinal considerations are certain to prevail.[16] The superstructure of bureaucratic control, provided for by the Polish decree, is thus necessary to maintain the priority of ideology over economics, at least in any foreseeable future.

But while recognizing that in the short run one cannot expect too much from pragmatic reforms now being introduced in Poland, one should not fail to acknowledge either the significant gains made by the protagonists of economic reforms, or the long-term potentialities of the proposed changes.

First of all, some of the postulates advocated by economic reformers have been included in the resolution of the IV Party Congress and as such have become an integral part of the official party program. The present party leadership in Poland (as elsewhere in the bloc) may not have the necessary political will to put this program into effect without adequate safeguards perpetuating the essentials of centralized control. But one has to bear in mind that the reforms which have been approved are objective and institutional, while the essence of the safety clauses is the subjective right of veto vested in the party leadership. What is needed to make those pragmatic reforms fully operative is thus a change of attitude of the people in power. The same thing is, to a certain degree, true of the Czechoslovak, the East German, and other reform blueprints. While a more positive attitude can hardly be expected from the Gomulkas, Ulbrichts, and Novotnys, there seems to be every likelihood of a less dogmatic approach as far as their eventual successors are concerned. Despite the built-in safeguards of bureaucratic control, these blueprints do create new institutional forms, which, given a more favorable political climate, may well become meaningful instruments for effecting a real change in the existing economic system.

This applies also to another Polish reform which concerns the methods of investment financing.[17] The essential objective of this

---

16 This point was made clear in the commentaries on the significance of the decree published in the party press. Cf. J. Szpt, "The Time of Reckoning," *Zycie Warszawy* (August 19, 1964).

17 The legal basis for this reform is the Decree of the Polish Council of Minis-

measure is to replace the traditional method of financing all investment projects, namely outright free grants, by repayable bank loans bearing a relatively high rate of interest.

In contrast to the fairly complicated provisions of the Decree of July 29, 1964, the modus operandi of the reform of investment financing is relatively simple and straightforward. The overall aim is to introduce the concept of the comparative economic effectiveness of alternative investment expenditures into an economic system where hitherto the political decision to invest has been the sole criterion.

To understand fully the real meaning of this reform, one has to realize what the method of investment financing, through bank credits bearing a fixed rate of interest, would mean from the point of view of an average factory manager in Poland, or for that matter in other countries of Eastern Europe.[18] Until now all new investment projects were paid for by an outright free grant from the state budget. Hence, from the point of view of the enterprise concerned, those investments did not cost anything. The question of whether the investment expenditure is necessary and justified was decided by central planners. But once such a decision was made, often in response to considerable political wirepulling by local party bigwigs,[19] the enterprise concerned was not charged a penny for the new capital it acquired. Naturally enough, this resulted in a constant tendency to over-invest, regardless of cost.

Under provisions of the Decree of March 10, 1965, the situation will change considerably. As a rule, all new investment projects at the enterprise level are to be financed by repayable bank loans, bearing a relatively high rate of interest (153). Thus, the factory manager must be prepared to repay the total cost of new investments out of the future income of his enterprise. In essence, this means that "investment capital ceases to be a free good

---

ters, dated March 10, 1965. Its text was not published either in *Monitor Polski* or in *Dziennik Ustaw*. However, the main provisions of this measure were explained at length in an article in *Trybuna Ludu* (see 153).

18 A similar reform of investment financing has been introduced in other Moscow bloc countries. See Chapter 3 for more details.

19 This type of wirepulling and other sharp practices resorted to by local party dignitaries were discussed at length by Gomulka in his XIV Plenum speech. Cf. *Trybuna Ludu,* (December 8, 1963).

and becomes a commodity, which has a definite market price" (154).

This poses a problem—entirely new for a manager of a socialized enterprise—namely, whether the given investment expenditure is, from his point of view, an economic proposition or not. In other words, whether the proposed investment can be expected to bring adequate returns. This is exactly the same criterion on which any businessman in the West bases his own investment decisions. The criterion of objective economic effectiveness of the proposed investment expenditure.

It is easy to see what the basic aims are of this new method of investment financing. Obviously, the communist planners are gradually becoming aware that the ever-growing shortage of investment means forces them to allocate the scarce resources available to the most economically effective alternatives (154). If carried to its logical conclusion, this would mean that the investment policy would cease to be dictated by arbitrary decisions of the bureaucratic oligarchy, determined primarily by ideological and political considerations, and would be determined by effective demand. But the new methods of investment financing are evidently an outcome of yet another compromise. On one hand, they do comply with one of the basic demands of economic reformers by introducing the test of economic effectiveness into the national investment policy. On the other hand, the Polish decree explicitly excludes from such a test the so-called "priority investments," or such projects, "which are considered (by the party leadership, of course) to be of basic national interest." Those "priority investments" are still to be financed by the traditional method of outright free grants (153).

So, here again, we have an apparently rational reform, deliberately neutralized by a built-in safeguard, perpetuating the divine right of the ruling party oligarchy to go ahead with any investment project it considers necessary for purely doctrinal reasons. That is, after all, the real meaning of the escape clause which the decree provides for all "priority investments."

But in assessing the practical results of this exemption one has again to distinguish between the long-term and short-term effects. As long as the generation of "professional revolutionaries" remains firmly in power, the escape clause will, no doubt, be used extensively to exempt any pet investment scheme favored by the dogmatic majority in the party leadership from the test of economic effectiveness. Thus in practice there would be two categories of investment projects in every national plan. One would be based on the principle of the most rational utilization of the available capital resources, and the other dictated by purely doctrinal considerations.

In the long run, however, the effects may well be different. The very fact that the test of economic efficiency in respect to some investment projects has been introduced into the system, where so far the arbitrary doctrinal considerations have reigned supreme, is certainly a significant breakthrough. Besides, for a new generation of party leaders, which are bound to suceed the Gomulkas (as well as the Novotnys, Ulbrichts, Kadars and Zhivkovs), the escape clause in the rules of investment financing, as the right of veto in respect to rational production decisions, may well lose their present doctrinal significance. One must always remember that the effectiveness of any rear-guard action depends essentially on the political strength and tenacity of the dogmatic elements. And in Poland (as elsewhere in the bloc) this dogmatic establishment is either slowly dying out or is being gradually pushed into political oblivion.

But in the meantime, in Poland at least, the adherents of centralist planning and bureaucratic control still have the upper hand. This was made clear when the Central Committee Plenum convened in July 1965 to approve the reform measures which the party leadership intends to introduce in Poland in 1966–70 (see 194). An obvious indication of the prevailing neo-dogmatic approach was the introductory speech delivered by Poland's Chief Planner, Stefan Jedrychowski (193).

The key passage of his speech had to do with the role of prices in the new economic model, and here he took an essentially conservative position. According to Jedrychowski the central authorities should maintain the permanent control of prices as an instrument of state policy. Prices should be manipulated in the service of long-run aims, such as a gradual change in the structure of consumption and also for short-term purposes such as adjusting demand to the available supply (an orthodox communist usage handed down from Stalin's day). "In no case," Jedrychowski stressed, "can we agree to a free movement of prices uncontrolled by the state, or to a spontaneous shaping of prices by . . . supply and demand" (193).

If the Polish leadership remained conservative and orthodox on the essential issue of prices, what did all these much-advertised changes amount to? Jedrychowski listed them as follows:

1) An undefined "deepening" of the scientific bases of planning, which should help to make better use of "science and technique in planning" and of "economic analysis."

2) Better cost accounting. But he gave no indication that considerations of economic effectiveness would prevail.

3) Alternative versions of the same plan, to allow enterprises more flexibility. Jedrychowski devoted much time to enumerating the advantages that would accrue to enterprises and plants from working out these "planning variants."

4) Continuity and flexibility of planning. Regarding the former, Jedrychowski suggested a number of improvements designed to ensure that plans for successive periods overlap each other, so that production could flow smoothly and not surge at the end of one period and decline at the beginning of another. With regard to flexibility, he stated that it would be only realistic to make plans flexible enough to reflect a) climatic conditions affecting agricultural production, b) changes in world market prices, and c) changing demand on the home market.

5) Adaptation of production to changing demand. This seemed to contradict what he had already said about prices and "price policy." However, the proposed expansion of various market research projects suggests that the intention is serious (193).

The final resolution of the CC Plenum referred vaguely to the need to replace "global production indices" with "new, more perfect" ones. But instead of spelling out what these ought to be, the resolution said merely that they would require "intensive work and experimentation" and that the "solution of the problem cannot be uniform in all branches of production" for "various methods are needed depending on the conditions of a given branch of the economy" (195).

There is obviously a wide disparity between the principles which the Polish leadership apparently endorsed in the summer of 1964 and the resolutions of the Fourth Plenum a year later.

Even practical measures sometimes lead to naught. That seems to have happened, for instance, with the July 1964 Decree on organizational and institutional changes in industry. Although this decree had deadlines for implementation of its provisions (none of them longer than twelve months), an official investigation carried out in the fall of 1965 disclosed that "90 percent of the individual enterprises and 70 percent of the industrial associations have so far failed to receive the necessary directives on how to proceed with the changes. . . . And so nothing has been done for lack of appropriate instructions" (139).

This shows how easily even a concrete and progressve legislative measure can be sabotaged. In Poland's centralized bureaucracy it is not really necessary for opponents of such a measure to take counteraction. It is often enough if they fail to issue the appropriate instructions to lower echelons.

Such delaying tactics cannot be pursued indefinitely. The leadership of the party has committed itself to carrying out all the reforms outlined in the resolution of the Fourth Plenum, and by the end of 1970. Barring the unforeseeable they will probably be implemented. But the real question is how the rather broad principles underlying those reforms will be interpreted in practice.

Professor Brus, one of the main protagonists of economic reforms in Poland, wrote at the beginning of 1966 that the real proof of change in the economic system is the character of the macro-economic decisions, which are as much political as economic. Therefore, he argued, the meaningful reforms of any economic system depend ultimately upon the changes in the functioning of the political institutions (145). Given the immobility of the political situation in Warsaw, and the essentially conservative attitude of the top party establishment, the pioneers of economic pragmatism in Poland have every reason to feel frustrated.

3

★

THE REVISIONIST TIDE OVERRUNS EASTERN EUROPE

The ups and downs of economic pragmatism in Poland may well be considered a clinical example of the inevitable frustrations which the more progressive elements in the Soviet bloc have to face when they attempt to introduce some degree of rationality into the existing economic system. Today, when nearly all countries of Eastern Europe including the Soviet Union have accepted, at least in principle, the need for extensive reforms, one may well pose the question: why was Poland, in the mid-fifties, so far ahead of the rest of the field?

In the introductory chapter I have already indicated the main factors which played their part in bringing about a decisive change in the approach to economic reforms. But the fact remains that the impact of all those factors was more or less the same throughout the whole bloc. The reason why their combined effect on Poland was so much stronger, at such an early date, can only be explained by one specific feature: the great weakness of the party political apparatus in the period following the events of October 1956.[1] Poland's premature political destalinization[2] and the spontaneous emergence of powerful social forces, which, for all practical

---

[1] A similar pragmatic effort in Hungary, which began in 1953–54 during the first premiership of Imre Nagy and continued in 1956–57 after the Kadar restoration, was nipped in the bud by the opposition of the party establishment.

[2] Poland's security apparatus was effectively neutralized in 1955 by the defection of Col. Swiatlo and his subsequent revelations. At the same time the new party leadership, elected in October 1956, was opposed by a substantial part of the existing apparatus.

purposes, have temporarily overthrown the entrenched dogmatic party establishment,[3] have created especially favorable conditions for an outbreak of economic nonconformity. As soon as the party power was effectively restored, however, the roll-back process began. But apart from a different internal situation, there were other objective economic and political factors which delayed the surfacing of revisionist thinking in the rest of the bloc for several years. Professor Brus, in an unusually outspoken article, defined those factors as "doctrinal obstacles" and slight economic gains which resulted from "taking advantage of the mistakes of the past period" (143). To make these points clear I would like to quote from his article:

> In the first stage of the post-Stalin period, the mounting frustration due to negative economic results was not always and not everywhere combined with a criticism of the centralized model as such and with a more basic revaluation of certain principles of economic policy of the past period. This was due to several doctrinal obstacles, as well as to reasons which belong to the field of the sociology of political relations. All these factors notwithstanding, in the very course of economic processes, facts appeared which—with a certain dose of wishful thinking—were supposed to indicate that the old system of planning and management could be usefully retained without any meaningful changes. The reason for this was that the economic policies and the totalitarian system, which prevailed during the last years of the Stalin era, so greatly hampered the rational exploitation of the economic potential, particularly in respect to consumer goods production and agriculture, that it was enough to correct the most glaring mistakes to achieve substantial positive effects. To this one has to add the production gains resulting from the fact that many enterprises, the construction of which was started in the previous period, have belatedly become operative. The economic cost of constructing these enterprises was extremely high, but it was already borne in the past. It had no effect on the current period. The cumulative result was that the institutional factors hampering the rate of growth have not become fully apparent.
>
> The five-year period 1956–1960 (and especially the period ending with 1959), was characterized in most socialist countries by a rapid rate of economic development, only little below in general indices

[3] The political situation in Poland after October 1956 is fully described by Flora Lewis (197); see also K. Syrop (198).

(such as the rate of growth of national income) from the rate of increase in the period immediately preceding it. It was also much more positive from the point of view of output of consumer goods. These were undeniably the circumstances which made it easier to negate the very need for, or at least delay of, the introduction of the more essential changes in the Economic Model. (143)

However, the respite was only temporary. By 1960 stagnation had set in and the overall economic situation began to deteriorate rapidly:

Already in the last phase of the period 1956–1960, a number of signs appeared indicating that "taking advantage of the mistakes of the past period" could not continue much longer. This became even clearer in the course of implementation of the 1961–1965 plans. One must not, naturally, disregard the achievements of that period, but one must not close one's eyes to the astonishing failures. They were apparent not only in the declining rate of growth of national income in all the European socialist countries (with the exception of Rumania) as compared with the previous period, but above all in the lower than expected effectiveness of investments (failure of several important indices of the plan despite the implementation and, in certain cases, the exceeding of the planned investment expenditures).

Nor does it seem accidental that the sharpest decline in the rate of growth took place in the most advanced socialist countries. In Czechoslovakia, the average annual rate of increase in the period 1961–1965 was 1.8 per cent, as compared to 7.0 per cent in the previous period, while in the GDR, the analogical figures were 2.8 per cent and 8.1 per cent. (143)

It was precisely this economic stagnation which provided the main impetus to the upsurge of more pragmatic thinking throughout the rest of the bloc. Unlike in Poland five or six years earlier, it was not the weakness of the party's political apparatus, but dire economic necessity which was the primary factor in bringing the revisionist reform proposals into the open. Soon there was a general agreement (at least in principle) that changes in the existing economic system could no longer be avoided.

The turning point in the tide of economic revisionism was the publication in *Pravda* of the now-famous article by Professor Liberman and the discussion of his ideas by Soviet economists (215). The discussion was carried out with the cautious approval of Khrushchev, who later endorsed some of Liberman's concepts (222). Their essence was the adoption of the profit motive as the mainspring of all economic activity. Professedly, Liberman sought only to improve the functioning of the existing system. His avowed goals were modest: he wanted to stimulate Soviet enterprises to seek higher output and to correlate their production with the needs of consumers; he wanted to encourage the introduction of new technology and new products, and to improve the quality of output. But in his critical appraisal of the system he effectively pinpointed its economic irrationality, its wastefulness, and its inflexibility.

Actually, "Libermanism" implies much more than its protagonists in the Soviet Union are prepared to say openly.[4] If carried to its logical conclusion, it would require no less than the abolition of centralized planning with its system of administrative directives, the adoption of profit as the basis for measuring economic efficiency, and the introduction of those elements of a market mechanism without which the profit motive cannot be fully effective. Thus the essential—if implicit—concepts of "Libermanism" are the same as those of the Polish economic model discussed in the previous chapter.

But the real political importance of the Libermanist ideas was that they have given economic pragmatism a more respectable status throughout the Soviet bloc. The publication of excerpts from the Soviet economic debate in *Pravda* and the endorsement, however, cautious, of certain pragmatic concepts by Khrushchev himself, has certainly made an impression on Ulbricht, Novotny, and Zhivkov. The great wave of economic revisionism in Eastern Europe followed closely on the heels of the early Soviet publications and the permissive attitude toward those mildly revisionist proposals adopted by Khrushchev.

The intellectual climate for this outbreak of economic pragmatism was created by the tide of political destalinization which swept Czechoslovakia, Bulgaria, and Hungary in the closing

[4] "Libermanism" is used here in a sense which became accepted in the West although the author is well aware that the actual contribution of Professor Liberman to pragmatic economic thinking in the Soviet Union is much smaller than of such economists as Kantorovich, Atlas, Nyemchinov, Gatovsky, and Trapeznikov.

months of 1962. This tide resulted, one way or another, in the removal of the more dogmatic elements from party leadership and generated popular pressure for further reform. The sudden upsurge of economic pragmatism in Eastern Europe is part and parcel of this popular pressure. The immediate aim seems to be to make the existing system more efficient. But as we have already seen the political and economic implications go much further.

After these general remarks, one may now examine the development of the pragmatic approach within the Soviet bloc, country by country. Since the post-1960 economic stagnation was the most pronounced in Czechoslovakia, one should not be surprised that the most dynamic changes in official thinking have come in that country. The first stage was one of public criticisms of the existing system, spurred on by the symptoms of economic crisis. Radoslav Selucky argued that the "cult of the plan" had been a manifestation of stalinism just as insidious as "the cult of personality" (44). This theme was taken up by other Czechoslovak economists, and the lively debate which ensued was followed by an overall attack on economic dogmatism in a series of three articles by Eugen Loebl (33), and a semi-official self-criticism in the party theoretical journal entitled "The Survivals of Dogmatism in Political Economy Must Be Overcome," by Ota Sik, director of the Economic Institute of the Czechoslovak Academy of Sciences (45), who later became the main protagonist of the Czechoslovak new economic model.

This discussion, however, centered on the theme of dogmatic errors in economic management and the reasons for the malfunctioning of the Czechoslovak economy. Although several voices had a strong revisionist accent, they did not go further than to invoke a set of general principles; no specific proposals were made for concrete reforms.

Much more fruitful in this respect was a round-table conference organized by the economic weekly *Hospodarske Noviny* which printed excerpts of the proceedings in November 1963. This conference undoubtedly broadened the scope and direction of the pragmatic trend, since it produced criticisms of the traditional system as such and not merely of its dogmatic abuses. Selucky argued that the law of supply and demand should apply not only to the sphere of consumer goods but to the entire economy. Milan

Plachky attacked the dogma of priority for the production of capital goods. Several speakers argued that planning should be regarded as a means to an end and not an end in itself. Finally, Zdenek Haba, head of the Department of Political Economy at the University of Bratislava, demanded the right to criticize the system as such and not merely the symptoms of its malfunctioning.

Although even the most audacious participants did not go beyond the formulation of certain basic principles, and the discussion was far less specific than the Liberman debate in the Soviet Union, its general implication was that of a return to the conditions of a market economy and all that this concept implies. The impact of such ideas has been manifested even in official party circles. On January 8, 1964 an editorial in *Rude Pravo* conceded cautiously that "production should be exposed to a certain amount of pressure both from the market and from the customers." On April 24 the Commission for Living Standards set up by the party Central Committee announced that "a new planning method is to be tried out in a number of selected factories." The basic criterion of efficiency was to be profitability.

Nevertheless, by the middle of 1964 Czechoslovakia was still one of the stragglers. The pragmatic debate seemed to be purely theoretical, centering on the theme of past errors in planning and management and on the reasons for the poor current performance of the economy. No concrete proposals for economic reform had yet been publicly formulated and no significant pilot experimental projects were in operation. But within a few months the situation had changed radically. By the end of 1964 a comprehensive blueprint for economic reform had been worked out and published. In January 1965 this was approved in principle by the Central Committee of the party. It was to become fully operative—at least so far as its basic principles were concerned—in 1966. Czechoslovakia thus skipped much of the tentative experimentation which the other countries are passing through and kept theoretical discussions to a minimum (see 84). In contrast to the East German policy of "small steps," Czechoslovakia has made "a great leap forward."

Let us take a closer look at the timetable of Czechoslovak economic reform. The blueprint of the new economic model was made public in October 1964 (70). After a three-month delay—

apparently because of political and ideological strife within the communist establishment—the party's Central Committee met on January 27–29 and formally adopted the principles of the new economic model, as expressed in the draft proposal (71). This meant that the party hierarchy had officially committed itself on the side of economic pragmatism. Detailed guidelines were to be issued by June 1965 and all problems concerning practical implementation were to be ironed out by the end of the year.

In February 1965 the theoretical and practical problems were discussed in great detail by the leading economists at a special five-day seminar.[5] The chief advocates of reform, led by Professor Ota Sik, were apparently not satisfied with what had been accomplished and continued to press for a broadening of the practical scope of the measures to which the party hierarchy was already committed in principle. They pursued this strategy throughout 1965, with particular emphasis on the need for a major shake-up in the top echelons of industrial management (see 34, 43, and Chapter 6).

The opponents of the new economic model were equally active. Like their counterparts in other countries, they avoided frontal attacks and theoretical disputes and concentrated instead on delaying tactics. Since the opponents of the reforms always operate behind the scenes, often paying lip-service to the need for a change, they are hard to identify. But they play on the inevitable fears and internal hesitations of party leaders and are, more often than not, successful. In Czechoslovakia they seem to have succeeded in slowing down the implementation of the new economic model. The January 1965 resolution stated that the basic principles of the new system were to be introduced in 1966, but later pronouncements called for their implementation in two stages. The first, beginning January 1, 1966, was to "create incentives for discovering material and labor reserves on the enterprise level." The second stage—from January 1967 onward—was to provide the solutions for "the problems of investments and the development of enterprises." The precise meaning of these terms is not clear, but the new formulation obviously implied a delay. This was confirmed by the official explanation that such "gradualism" is neces-

[5] See *Politicka Ekonomie* (April 1965).

sary because numerous practical problems and disproportions do not permit a speedier implementation of the new economic model.[6]

Yet another regressive development was the resolution adopted by the Central Committee early in November 1965. This reiterated that the initial reforms envisaged by the new economic model would go into effect on January 1, 1966, but the concrete measures it indicated were purely organizational (74). Their main thrust is to shift the work of the central government from operative economic direction to long-range perspective planning. The responsibility for solving concrete questions of production is to rest with individual enterprises and the industrial associations.

While this meant a decentralization of economic decision-making, as called for in the blueprint, the actual extent of the changes was still rather hazy. Broadly speaking, one could well assume that general economic policy questions would remain the exclusive prerogative of central institutions, while some of the other economic decisions (wages, prices, assortment of products) would be made at a lower level. But exactly what these latter will comprise was not indicated in the resolution.

One of the basic issues at stake was the determination of prices, wage rates, and employment limits at the enterprise level. The blueprint published in October 1964 provided for a major reform of the existing price system. It foresaw three categories of prices: state-determined prices for basic raw materials and the fundamental necessities of life; state-controlled prices for most other goods, which would be permitted to fluctuate within the upper and lower limits established periodically by the central planners, and a free price system for certain categories of consumer goods (57).[7]

This made good economic sense as long as actual determination of prices in the last two categories was left to individual enterprises or at least to the trusts. The blueprint also implied quite clearly (although this was not spelled out in the text) that the managers of enterprises would be able to regulate employment and set their own wage rates, as had been assumed by most Czechoslovak reformers (see 84, 85).

---

[6] *Prace* (September 10, 1965).

[7] The Czechoslovak (and the Hungarian) "three category price system" is discussed in more detail in Chapter 4.

The outcome may be otherwise. The November 1965 resolution stated that a new central institution—the State Commission for Finance, Prices, and Wages—was to be established, although it did not specify the powers which were to be granted to the new body. The commission may, of course, confine itself to fixing the prices of raw materials and other essentials and to setting the limits for the prices that are to be allowed to fluctuate. This would be fully consistent with the principles of the New Economic Model. But there are strong indications (in some of Novotny's speeches, for instance) that the party hierarchy does not intend to abdicate much of its power over prices and wages.[8] And the new central body would be a perfect instrument for retaining control of them.

Thus on the eve of the implementation of the preliminary measures of the new economic model, the situation in Czechoslovakia conformed to the well-known pattern: on one side a truly pragmatic blueprint envisaging really far-reaching reforms, on the other an apparent lack of political will to carry those reforms to their logical conclusion. "The central authorities," warned a Slovak economist, "are already looking for possibilities of limiting the freedom of action of the enterprises by a system of additional obligations, which can be enforced by a variety of means" (27). This undercover tug of war persisted throughout 1966 and the chief protagonists of the new economic model openly expressed their dismay over the slow progress of the reforms (32).[9] And, although the 13th Congress of the Czechoslovak Comunist Party in June 1966 unanimously approved all the pragmatic principles

[8] In his report to the Central Committee on November 3, Novotny stated: "It is necessary to emphasize once more that it is impossible to permit any kind of arbitrariness in the development of wages and that the material interests and reward for work must be unconditionally bound to the satisfaction of society's needs. . . . The government must apply its authority, and by its activity must safeguard for the Party the realization of the political and economic aims involved in the development of our country." The Commission for Finance, Prices, and Wages must "play a significant role" in the "coordination of all basic questions of financial loan, price and wage policy." It "will also guide the execution of wage and price policy within the broader confines of the development of living standards, the balance of revenues and expenditures of the population, and the development of the incomes of the people and the enterprises" (74).

[9] Loebl's opinions expressed in this article are quoted at length in Chapter 5.

of the new system of planning and management, the advocates of radical reforms were not too optimistic (80). "The chief obstacle," warned Professor Sik in an interview published in the Slovak trade union daily, *Praca,* "is the non-economic way of thinking of some people who are backing the new system with words, but in practice follow the old ways" (50).

Despite all this resistance, however, there was some progress. At the end of July 1966 the Prague regime published detailed instructions and explanatory notes which were to serve as a guide for launching the new economic model in enterprise management on 1 January 1967 (81). It had also been decided to begin the reform of the wholesale price system on the same date and the country was soon swept by rumors of a forthcoming increase in retail prices as well.[10] Indeed some upward adjustment in respect to the prices of meat and beer were announced early in October 1966,[11] but they were allegedly fully balanced by price cuts in other foodstuffs.[12] The Czechoslovak authorities denied that a general increase of the retail prices was contemplated in the near future, but warned that "some upward readjustments in certain categories of prices cannot be avoided" (37). It was clear that some hardships were certainly in the offing, at least for the initial stages of the new economic model and the reformers appealed to the people not to put the blame for short term negative consequences on the new system (52). Thus the Czechoslovak people entered the first phase of the New Economic Model without illusions of a paradise around the corner and bracing themselves for the initial shocks of higher prices and possible dislocations in employment.

Such open warnings about the possible side effects of economic reforms were unheard of in East Germany, where the changes in planning and management were imposed from above without the preliminary stage of public debates, as was the case in the rest of the bloc. On the other hand the pragmatic changes are being intro-

---

10 *Lidova Demokracie* (October 2, 1966).

11 *Rude Pravo* (October 2, 1966).

12 According to *Praca,* the net result of all these price adjustments is to increase the average family expenditure on food by 0.1 to 0.6 per cent, depending on the consumption pattern. The increase in price of meat (ranging from 5.8 per cent for pork to 11.7 per cent for veal) was explained by supply shortages and an "intolerable cost" of increasing imports (October 2, 1966).

duced by the Ulbricht regime with the typical German thoroughness in a step-by-step fashion. In many respects economic reforms are perhaps further advanced in East Germany than in Czechoslovakia (or anywhere else in the bloc for that matter), but the long-run outlook is less radical. The Ulbricht blueprint was published in July 1963, fifteen months before that of Czechoslovakia (90). It has been scrupulously implemented, with an emphasis on organizational decentralization rather than on more incentives at the factory level.

The decentralization consists of transferring certain basic economic decisions to industrial associations (93). Each of these groups, called a Vereinigung Volkseigener Betriebe, is really an independent economic unit or is intended to develop into one. It receives only a minimum of directive indicators from the central authorities, and is thus a kind of semi-independent industrial concern. (The Polish industrial association, by contrast, lacks this independence and is still mainly an administrative unit.)

Their decision-making power has devolved to the Vereinigungen Volkseigener Betriebe from the industrial departments of the National Economic Council and the State Planning Commission. At the same time, the VVB's have become the task-setters for a large number of subsidiary industrial enterprises. In effect, there has been in East Germany a two-directional shift of the focal point of economic decision making toward the VVB's—downward from the central agencies and upward from the individual factories. However, some enterprises are still to remain directly responsible to the industrial departments of the National Economic Council, or subject to the local control of the Bezirk (district) economic councils.

Apart from these substantial organizational changes, the pragmatic measures introduced so far in East Germany have been far less dramatic than those anticipated in the Czechoslovak new economic model. Nevertheless, by following its own method of small practical steps, East Germany has forged well ahead in the actual implementation of pragmatist rules of the game. The list of reform measures already introduced or envisaged for the future is long and varied. Capital assets have been revalued. Depreciation rates have been reassessed. Interest rates have been introduced. Subsidies have been reduced. Profits, like bonuses, are being related to performance and individual contracts are taking the place of centrally determined allocations. Last, but not least, the price system is being overhauled. "*Tonnen-ideologie*" (tonnage ideology) is to be replaced by a method based on accounting in financial rather than physical terms.[13]

Profits are to be related to net output rather than to gross production in an effort to eliminate the waste of materials which the previous system encouraged. Except for major projects which require the approval of the Council of Ministers, investment decisions are to rest in the future with the directors of the new industrial trusts. The central investment bank is to restrict its supervisory function to financial matters and to leave production decisions to industrial managers. Plan targets are to be limited to essentials so as to leave industrial enterprises some room for maneuver. Reductions in cost and improvements in quality are to be given priority over volume and weight of output.

With such a degree of pragmatism in other fields, the East German regime remained for a long time emphatically conservative on the basic issue. It insisted on preservation of the principle of central price control. Although in the original Ulbricht blueprint prices had been assigned a special role as "economic levers," their determination was indicated by their remaining the exclusive prerogative of the central planners (90). As late as December 1965, Ulbricht still insisted that the adaptation of prices to the prevailing market conditions had to be achieved "in a planned way," i.e., by central planners (92). Nevertheless, Ulbricht did admit the need for "greater flexibility of prices within industry" as long as they followed "socially necessary expenditures for production."

However, this rigid attitude to the price system underwent a significant change at the end of 1966. In an article which appeared in the Soviet economic weekly *Ekonomicheska Gazieta*, an East German economist spoke about the adoption of four categories of prices: a) "fixed prices"; b) "maximum prices"; c) "calculated prices," established by the enterprise on the basis of instructions and in cooperation with state price-determining agencies; and d)

---

13 The most extensive analysis of the various small steps toward economic pragmatism undertaken by the Ulbricht regime can be found in "Economic Reforms in East Germany" by D. Miller and Harry G. Trend (94).

"contract prices," determined by the buyer and seller (89, p. 39). While a more detailed analysis of the East German proposals concerning the flexible price system is in the next chapter, one may say here that the proposed changes are certainly symptomatic of the generally more flexible approach to economic reform now being undertaken by East Germany. One must include the increased planning authority of the Bezirk in local economic matters, the newly gained participation in plan trade unions, the development of "partnership councils" as a means of reducing the monopoly controls of VVB's, and the expansion of the role of the banks in the field of finance, all at the expense of the VVB where economic power had been enhanced substantially in 1963.

Unlike the other East European countries, the GDR has arrived at recognizing the importance of this need for increased flexibility on the basis of a general application of several segments of what is now called the new economic model and therefore the improved responsiveness of the economic management system represents the fruit of practical experience.

In Hungary the story is different. As far as the officially approved blueprints are concerned, Budapest has joined the leading group of East European economic pragmatists very late in the game.[14] However, preliminary discussion on the need for economic reforms began in Hungary even earlier than in Poland. Already in 1953–54, during the first Premiership of Imre Nagy, the Hungarian economists drafted a plan of reform similar to the one now being carried out in Czechoslovakia. After the 1956 revolt, when Kadar was busy "liquidating the counter-revolution," he called upon some of the leading economists to work out a new program which would avoid the mistakes of former years. The government set up eleven committees of experts and in the summer of 1957 they presented their conclusions, which bore a strong resemblance to the ideas now being accepted in other countries. Their proposals, however, encountered opposition in some party quarters where they were considered too right wing, and nothing was done about them (134).

In 1965 Kadar turned to the economists again, and again eleven

[14] The Hungarian Central Committee approved the blueprint of the new economic model in late May 1966. Cf. *Nepszabadsag* (May 29, 1966).

committees were set up. The Central Committee discussed their recommendations in November—reportedly there was an "extensive debate"—and agreed to work out practical measures on the basis of their proposals.[15] After another six months of preparatory work, the Central Committee met again (May 25–27, 1966) and the reform blueprint received the formal approval of the Hungarian Socialist Workers Party. According to the resolution adopted at this meeting, the most important changes to be introduced gradually until 1968 are: a) new principles of planning and management that will give a greater independence to directors of enterprises; b) a new system of wages and prices in which the essentials of centralized control are to be combined with a degree of flexibility granted to individual enterprises; c) greater attention is to be paid to the needs of the market and effective demand is to be reflected in the production plans; and d) all the existing bureaucratic superstructure between the level of the ministries and that of individual enterprises is to be abolished.[16]

Apart from the usual verbiage and the obligatory set of new economic principles, the Hungarian blueprint contained four distinct features: first of all, the proposed new model was to be applied not only in industry and the distributive services but also in agriculture.[17] Secondly, a new "three category" price system (not unlike that which was adopted in Czechoslovakia) was to be established.[18] Thirdly, unlike Poland, Czechoslovakia, and East Germany, the Hungarian blueprint did not foresee the creation of a middle-level superstructure in the industrial sector in the form of trusts or industrial associations. Thus, the degree of independence granted to the enterprise directors appeared to be greater than elsewhere in the bloc.[19] Finally, the Hungarians were the first to realize that in the changed conditions of the new economic model,

---

15 See the Hungarian press agency MTI's report on the Plenum, November 20, 1965 and *Nepszabadsag* (November 21, 1965).

16 Cf. the text of the CC Plenum resolution published in *Nepszabadsag* (May 29, 1966), see also "Hungary—Iron Out of Wood" by Joseph Held (136).

17 The basic measures of the Hungarian agricultural reform are discussed in Chapter 9.

18 Hungarian price proposals are analyzed in Chapter 4.

19 The great importance of this structural change will be apparent to the reader after he has read Chapter 5 on the pitfalls of half-way decentralization.

the role of the trade unions would have to undergo significant reassessment.[20]

One of the essential characteristics of the Hungarian reform—and this was especially emphasized by Rezso Nyers in his keynote speech—is the establishment of a relationship between the active role of the market and the central direction of the national economy. The central organ is to fix only the long-term tasks to be fulfilled, but the details of these tasks will be set by the enterprises themselves according to the market requirements. It will be the duty of the superior organs to harmonize these market requirements and national interests.[21]

The independence of individual enterprises will increase considerably. In practical terms, this means the end of the traditional system of economic direction. In the past the enterprises received an obligatory plan, broken down for them individually, which had to be fulfilled. In the future they will prepare their own plan themselves, being obliged to take into consideration market requirements and effective demand. Instead of direct intervention, the state will use indirect economic means (credit, price and interest policy, etc.) to influence the decisions of individual enterprises.

The enterprises will have greater freedom to establish their own wage policy. Under the old economic regime, the wage system has been almost identical throughout the country, while in the future the income of workers and employees will differ from enterprise to enterprise. This is intended to be an incentive, for income—particularly that of the enterprise leadership—will depend on the results of the profit and loss account of individual enterprises. The enterprise will retain a considerable part of its profit after the deduction of taxes and the shares due to the state. Out of this remaining profit the management could improve the wages and set up a reserve fund. The resolution stated that in the future emphasis will have to be placed on real wages (as distinct from social allotments) as the main means of improving living standards; there will have to be a proportionally greater increase in real wages than heretofore (130).

---

20 This topic is extensively discussed in Chapter 8.

21 Cf. Rezso Nyers' speech as reported in *Nepszabadsag* (July 26, 1966).

The decisive sphere of the new economic system was to be the reform of prices. Prices will have to reflect faithfully the real value of an article. There will be different categories of prices. Some of the prices will be fixed by the state and will be binding in character, while part of them will be freely formed by the enterprises according to the law of demand and supply. In a restricted form some competition among enterprises will also be permitted. It was also stated that the increase of wage level must surpass the increase of price level. The preparation of the new price system was to begin forthwith and the new system was to become effective as of January 1, 1968.

As elsewhere in the bloc, the Hungarian reform proposals met with an obstinate resistance of the entrenched dogmatic elements. This rear-guard action was publicly acknowledged by the Italian communist party official weekly *Rinascita* as coming from "extremists" who were afraid that the reforms may undermine the "leading role of the Hungarian Party in the economic life of the country and in evolving a new social system" (137, p. 9). Such doubts were confirmed indirectly when the official Hungarian party daily *Nepszabadsag* published the speech made by Politburo member Jeno Fock, who emphasized that the Party will retain "its leading role" throughout the implementation of the economic reform (102).

Although in Hungary the actual blueprint of the new economic model has been worked out relatively late by East European standards, in one respect the economy was well prepared for reform. For several years the Kadar regime has been removing incompetent party hacks from leading positions in the economic apparatus and replacing them by qualified managerial personnel, more often than not by non-party specialists. Since the caliber of the people who will be putting the reforms into effect is at least as important as the economic content of those reforms, one can say that in this respect Hungary has already prepared the ground.

While Czechoslovakia and Hungary passed directly from the phase of theoretical discussions to one of a comprehensive macroeconomic blueprint, Bulgaria followed the Soviet way of scattered micro-economic experiments. Also, apart from a few substantive articles on the subject of economic reform, there was little evidence of theoretical discussion. One of the earliest manifestations of pragmatic theoretical thinking was an article by Professor A. Miloshevsky in the November 1963 issue of *Novo Verme* (3) in which the adoption of the Yugoslav model, including co-management of enterprises by workers' councils and profit-sharing schemes, was cleary advocated. But far more significant, both in economic as well as in political terms, was another article published in *Novo Vreme* a month later and written by the then recently rehabilitated Kostovite, Professor Petko Kunin.[22]

This contribution is highly important, if only because with it economic revisionism has entered Bulgaria by the front door—in the form of an article published in the official theoretical monthly of the Bulgarian communist party and written by a member of the Central Committee (1).

Professor Kunin's article was devoted to the problem of economic incentives as the mainspring of all economic activity. In itself, the concept of economic incentives had, by that time, become quite respectable: even Khrushchev advocated their use from time to time. But prudent party officials still preferred to talk about this delicate subject in noncommittal generalities. Not so Professor Kunin, who made it clear from the beginning that one cannot expect economic incentives to work effectively within the framework of the existing system of planning and managing national industry. "Before one makes an appeal to the motive of material interest," he wrote, "one has to create conditions in which economic incentives can play their full part in stimulating the process of production" (1).

Starting from this basic premise, the Bulgarian economist went on to indicate the sweeping reforms necessary. Like many other Soviet bloc economists, Professor Kunin argued that the first thing to do is to free the individual enterprise from the shackles of centralized planning. He advocated making each individual enterprise an independent and self-supporting economic unit, working according to principles of full cost accounting. The management of such an independent enterprise should be given full control of

---

[22] Prof. Kunin received a fifteen-year jail sentence in the aftermath of Traicho Kostov's trial. Early in 1960 he was rehabilitated and at the VIII Party Congress in November 1962 reelected to the Central Committee of the Bulgarian communist party.

investment and marketing, subject only to general directives of the national planning authority.

But the main remedy Professor Kunin advocated for Bulgaria's economic ills was the old-fashioned medicine of competition. Socialized enterprises should compete with each other for the market, and the remuneration of both managers and workers should depend on the outcome of this competitive process. This would result in more, better, and cheaper production. At the same time, the consumer would get a better break.

Inevitably, Professor Kunin made the profit motive the mainspring of all economic activity. By incorporating the existing turnover tax, profit would return to its original definition as the difference between the selling price and the production cost per unit. The economic effectiveness of each enterprise would then no longer be measured in terms of total output, but in terms of the profit it makes. Profits would determine the remuneration of the managers and be the main source of increases in wage payments. He also advocated what amounted to a full-scale profit-sharing scheme in which all the staff of a given enterprise would participate, and which would supplement the workers' basic income. In this way, the workers' living standards would be linked to the economic effectiveness of the enterprise, and they would acquire a direct interest in its performance.

Most of Professor Kunin's ideas were sheer economic heresy in terms of orthodox Marxist doctrine. The fact that such revisionist ideas were published in the theoretical monthly of the Bulgarian communist party by a member of the Central Committee was proof that a new phase in Bulgarian economic policy was about to begin.

As could well be expected, the pragmatist practice in Bulgaria fell well short of Professor Kunin's maximalist postulates. Even before his article appeared in print, the necessary reform measures were discussed behind closed doors by the Bulgarian Politburo. In May 1963, Zhivkov presented to this body a report on the guidelines of a new system of planning and management. The report was never published, but apparently the Politburo discussed it at length and in January 1964 it was adopted "in principle" (16, p. 19).

Four months later the decision was made to try out the new

system through isolated micro-economic test cases. The experiment began in the Dimitrova woolen textile mill, subsequently expanding to about fifty enterprises in a number of industries. By late 1965 about 30 per cent of all major industrial establishments were reportedly involved, including most of light industry and food processing, as well as some machinery factories (10). The Bulgarians have also experimented with a regrouping of industry into industrial associations resembling those which have already been set up in other countries. Nine such trusts were apparently already in existence controlling the output and other activities of their subordinate enterprises.

Bulgarian experiments, both on the enterprise level and on that of the trust, were based on the principle of profitability and a certain degree of profit sharing. But the enterprises had no say in determining prices or wages, and had little authority in shaping the profile of production. To discourage unnecessary capital accumulation, the government had imposed a levy on all fixed and circulating capital (7).

On the basis of all those experiments, the Bulgarian Central Committee approved in December 1965 a draft proposal of a comprehensive reform blueprint at the time inviting a public discussion on the subject (11). The reforms outlined in this draft proposal followed a dual approach: centralized control on the macro-economic scale and indirect controls at the factory and trust level. The Bulgarians were also playing with the idea of a more elastic system of prices, although not to the extent adopted in Hungary and Czechoslovakia. On the whole, the proposed measures seemed promising though not as boldly conceived as in other countries. Experiments were to continue throughout 1966 and 1967, and beginning with 1968 the "new system" was to be applied to the whole economy.[23]

The proponents of more radical reforms took the advantage of the "open discussion period" to press their case. In January 1966, professor Georgi Petrov of the Karl Marx High Economic Institute published an article in *Rabotnichesko Delo*, which in effect amounted to a counter-proposal to the official Central Committee

[23] BTA reported on March 8, 1967 that 70 per cent of all industrial enterprises were working according to the new system.

Theses (6). Professor Petrov suggested among other things the abolition of the compulsory character of plan indices and free economic competition among independent enterprises, which would determine their own selling prices and wage rates. A few days later *Rabotnichesko Delo* published another article by Professor Anatas Lyutov, in which the suggestions of Petrov were severely criticized and condemned as a "total rejection of socialist planning" (2).

These open polemics were, however, only the visible part of the iceberg of reform controversy. Much more serious dispute raged apparently within the party establishment, but behind closed doors. The Central Committee Plenum, which was to give its final approval of the proposed draft, originally scheduled for the end of January 1966 (10) was twice postponed—the first time with an official announcement[24] and the second time silently. At long last the Central Committee met at the end of April 1966 when it "approved the basic principles of the new economic system" and entrusted the Politburo with the task of putting the final touches to the text of basic principles, "taking into account the report of comrade T. Zhivkov and the statements of the participants of the Plenum" (12). Thus the fight was not over yet.

The discussions on the theses, as well as Zhivkov's report at the Plenum, have revealed the existence of controversies and conflicts of competence between trusts and ministries, and monopolist approaches by the newly created trusts. It seems, however, that above all it was the problems of wages and prices and the wish of the regime at least partly to accommodate them to a modern market mechanism which were causing the greatest difficulties and headaches. Last but not least among the obstacles for the application of the new system were the conservative cadres who, as Zhivkov said, "continue to apply administrative methods" and do not re-adapt themselves to the new system.

On the key issue of prices, Zhivkov said that a complete reform of the system of price determination will be carried out, a promise which already had been made in the theses.[25] The new prices must be flexible, they must reflect the cost of production, and they must

24 *Rabotnichesko Delo* (January 26, 1966).
25 *Rabotnichesko Delo* (December 4, 1965).

represent a scientific measure of the labor involved. He also underlined that the new prices must do away with the discrepancy existing now between domestic prices and those on the international markets. How all this is to be achieved was obviously too early to say. Zhivkov said that these are problems on which it will be necessary to continue to work and the suggestions that will be made will have to be tested in practice.

All these difficulties probably explain the trend, as seen in Zhivkov's report, to stress administrative methods as opposed to economic levers, as for example through the introduction of state orders, increasing the role of the ministries, fixing limits for the flexibility of wages, etc. Much of this may indeed be only provisional and temporary, but it seemed that the Bulgarian regime was not yet prepared to apply a system which consisted of so many and important innovations and that it was afraid of losing the control over the economy by giving too much liberalization all at once. A group of about 150 specialists was to continue to work on improving the system and much still remained to be done, especially as the reorganization of the price system will hardly be ready to be tested before the middle of 1967.

However the Bulgarian model may evolve in the future, one thing seems to be certain. The crucial issue in Bulgaria, even more so than in the other countries, is that of maintaining the essential elements of party control over the economy. For a long time it has been clear that the party establishment intends not only to retain its present prerogatives, but to assume even wider ones (9). There are many indications that pressures of this kind have been a factor delaying the advance of economic pragmatism in Bulgaria (see 16, 17).

Within the general upsurge of economic pragmatism in Eastern Europe, Rumania remains a special case. Aside from a fragmentary reform of wholesale prices carried out back in 1963, there were, until the end of 1966, no signs of any meaningful attempt at economic reform in Rumania. Bucharest was apparently too busy with its energetic drive for political and economic independence and with building up a modern industrial base to pay serious attention to the issue of economic efficiency in its huge, modern (and more often than not Western-financed) industrial undertakings. The Rumanian indifference to pragmatic reforms also had an objective reason. The country was going through the process of rapid industrialization and from the point of view of the marginal returns on new investment outlays, it was at the same stage of economic development at which, say, Poland and Hungary were in the mid-fifties. Rumania's basic problem was, and still largely is, one of creating a modern industrial potential to balance off its essentially agricultural and raw material economy.

But during 1966, the question of getting a proper return on the invested capital and the dire necessity to adapt output to the competitive conditions in the Western markets forced the Rumanian leaders to revise, at least to some extent, their traditionalist indifferent attitude toward the problem of economic efficiency. In the second half of 1966, the Rumanian press published a series of articles stressing the necessity of a more pragmatic and rational attitude to the problems of planning and industrial management (see 205, 208, 209). It was specifically suggested to enlarge the competence of individual enterprises in the sphere of planning, investment, wage rates, and manpower. The weekly *Romania Libera* also proposed the establishment of a central institute to promote the introduction of scientific methods of management at the enterprise level. Another reform of wholesale prices also seemed to be in the offing. An article published in the October 1966 issue of the monthly *Probleme Econmice* recalled the reform of wholesale prices in 1963 and went on to reveal that those prices had been subsequently corrected so as to reduce excessive profits in certain branches of industry (206). The article advocated a new general readjustment of wholesale prices to promote greater economic efficiency.

All these proposals do not yet add up to a coherent whole. But they do show a growing awareness of the inadequacy of the existing economic system. The fact remains, however, that in contrast to other East European countries, no comprehensive blueprint for economic reforms has been elaborated in Rumania and no broad, open discussion of the problem involved has taken place. Yet it seems that some of the familiar elements of other reform programs are apparently under active consideration in Rumania.

More important still, a certain note of urgency crept into the discussion of more pragmatic solutions by the end of 1966. This was probably best illustrated by the speech which the Rumanian

First Secretary, Nicolae Ceausescu, delivered at the Central Committee Plenum at the end of December 1966 (210). Ceausescu was unusually severe in his criticism of the Rumanian industry. He frankly painted quite a bleak picture of the deficiencies which still prevailed after almost two decades of planned economy and announced that a whole series of problems—including improved organization of enterprises, the application of economic incentives, management training, and increased role of the banking system—would come up for consideration in 1967. Thus some significant changes along the standard lines of a more pragmatic approach can be expected in the near future.

In one respect Rumania enjoys an obvious advantage over all other East European countries. Its party leadership proved consistently to be far more susceptible to national interests of Rumania than to the dictates of Marxist ideology. One may thus well assume that once the political pragmatists of the Bucharest Politburo become convinced that further practice of economic dogmatism is prejudicial to Rumania's national interest, they would not hesitate to jettison some ideological principles for the sake of economic efficiency.

In contrast to this Rumanian pragmatism, the Soviet party establishment, both at the top and especially at the upper middle level, is essentially conservative and dogmatic in its outlook. In addition, the vested interests of the economic bureaucracy, which have grown during the half century of communist rule, are much more formidable than elsewhere in the bloc. Besides, the application of uniform economic reforms throughout the vast territory of the Soviet Union presents, no doubt, immense problems. These are just some of the factors which tend to delay the implementation of pragmatic solutions in the fatherland of communism. But when all this is said, the fact remains that economic reforms in the Soviet Union are still essentially at the stage of theoretical debates and scattered experiments. Nevertheless the overall trend of Soviet economic pragmatism leads unmistakably away from centralized planning based on directives from above, and toward a market economy where the chief incentive will be profit.

Such, at least, was the general tenor of the reform proposals outlined in the Kosygin report, delivered at the Central Committee Plenum in September 1965 (223, pp. 1–4). After long years of hesitation and backtracking, a partial green light was given for a tryout of some pragmatic solutions. The Kosygin report described the initial measures to be adopted and offered glimpses of broader reforms yet to come. But it has also demonstrated how far the Soviet Union has lagged behind most of the other European communist countries in its economic thinking and practice.

During the first decade after the war, the Soviet Union was the generally accepted model for the other countries. Now the roles have been reversed. First the Poles and Hungarians, and now the East Germans and Czechoslovaks, have pioneered new methods and ideas. The Russians have hung back, devoting vast energies to a rather tepid discussion of the ideas of Professor Liberman.[26]

The stage of theoretical discussion lasted longer in the Soviet Union than in any other country. The experiments, when they came, were confined at first exclusively to a small sector of the consumer goods industry. And the initial reforms announced in September 1965 fell short of the changes effected (or proposed) elsewhere in the bloc.

To be sure, the Kosygin report offered only a broad outline of the coming reforms. It represented, no doubt, a compromise—and a rather uneasy one—between two schools of thought. Indeed, to judge by the conflicting tendencies of the Kosygin report, the internal struggle over reform has been even more intense in the Soviet Union than in the other countries. Moreover, the conservatives and economic bureaucrats seem to have come out ahead in their defense of the essentials of central control (at least on the macro-economic scale).

Analyzing the potentially most important and critical area of economic reform, the pricing mechanism, one finds that the Soviet Union has opted for the most conservative solution. It is true that the plant manager will be able to make application for an increase (or decrease) in the price of his products. But as a rule all prices will continue to be fixed by the central authorities (see 223). And

26 The political significance of the Libermanist discussion on the Soviet Union has already been stressed in the introductory part of this chapter. A substantive account of the arguments and counterarguments which followed the publication of professor Liberman's article (215) would merely overburden the text. An excellent summary of Libermanist discussion can be found in "Economic Controversy in the Soviet Union" by Marshall Goldman (225).

there is apparently no intention of introducing variable and free prices as in Czechoslovakia, Hungary, and even Bulgaria or East Germany.[27]

Another doubtful step was the strengthening of central control at the ministerial level. This implied a stricter central direction of the industrial associations than elsewhere in the bloc. It involved the establishement of twenty-eight new industrial ministries to replace the fifty regional economic councils (sovnarkhozy) set up by Khrushchev in 1957. Of the new ministries, eleven were to be national bodies in charge of various branches of engineering and construction. The other seventeen were to be joint Union-Republic bodies working through similar organizations in the fifteen constituent republics. These will control the production of metals, fuel, oil and power, as well as mining and trade (see 223). Complicated and ambiguous as this structure is, it does seem to indicate an intention to retain a maximum of centralized control for the benefit of the highest echelons of economic bureaucracy. Matters look more promising at the micro-economic level. The new statute for Soviet enterprises seems to increase greatly both the prerogatives and the responsibilities of local managers, although the state frequently seems to give with one hand and take away with the other (224, pp. 25 ff.).

Thus managers are now able to retain a part of their profits for the purpose of offering incentives in the form of monthly and yearly bonuses to their workers (and themselves). The bonuses are to be fixed at a given percentage of profits. A fund—also a fixed part of profits—is to be set up for workers' housing. Management will be permitted to deal directly with customers and to base production plans and delivery schedules on those dealings—within the framework of the broad plan handed down by Gosplan. These innovations could spur the manager and his workers to greater efforts.

On the other hand, while the state will no longer tell the plant manager how many workers he can employ and what their productivity and average wage should be, he must still not exceed the total wage fund established for the factory. Moreover, although the state has stopped setting production targets for individual en-

[27] See Chapter 4 for more details of the proposed changes in price determination.

terprises (but not for industries) and has replaced them by sales targets in an effort to spur the manager to emphasize quality and pay more attention to consumers, the state will continue to decide what goods are to be produced and what raw materials are to be used.

Some interesting changes have been made in the control of investment. The enterprise will have to obtain money from the state in the form of long-term credits, and pay a levy on the value of its fixed assets. In the past when plants ran short of working funds the state automatically provided the necessary amount; now the plants will have to borrow. As all these new charges will have to come from enterprise funds, inefficiency will be penalized by lower profits.

The scope for initiative on the enterprise level is thus greater than before, but still quite limited. Significantly, the enterprises will not be given the degree of freedom accorded to the first experimental enterprises Mayak and Bolshevichka, particularly in the setting of prices and wages.[28]

Nevertheless the preliminary effects of the more pragmatic methods of management seemed to be encouraging. In May 1966, *Ekonomicheska Gazieta* drew up an initial balance sheet of the performance of forty-three experimental enterprises, which were the first to be transferred to the new system approved by the September 1965 Plenum (218, pp. 19 ff.). According to this preliminary progress report, in the first quarter of 1966 the experimental plants increased their sales by 12.4 per cent (as compared with 7.9 per cent average throughout the rest of industry) and have exceeded their planned profits for the first quarter of 1966 by 7.9 per cent. At the same time the labor productivity in the forty-three experimental factories increased by 6.5 per cent as against the 4.6 per cent of all industry average. Those figures themselves were not, perhaps, terribly impressive, since one has to

---

[28] In May 1964, Bolshevichka, a Moscow factory making men's clothing and Mayak, a Gorki enterprise producing women's dresses, became the first Soviet enterprises to be evaluated on something other than global quantity of output. To stimulate production of items better-suited to customers' needs, the payment of premiums was made dependent on the fulfillment of delivery and profit plans. The managers of the plants concerned were given extended prerogatives for adjusting wage rates and the size of the labor force.

bear in mind that the "all industry averages" which were used throughout as a standard of comparison included, of course, the performance of the most inefficient and uneconomic enterprises. Much more significant perhaps was the highly bullish and bombastic tenor of this preliminary progress report, with its "at all costs" emphasis on the positive effects of the new methods of management. One could not escape the impression that this preliminary report was really a sort of esoteric polemic with the conservative and dogmatic elements of the Soviet hierarchy and, as such, an indirect proof that the opposition to the reforms was still strong and widespread. This impression was further strengthened when the same emphatic statements about the superior performance of experimental enterprises appeared with monotonous regularity in almost every routine report on the performance of Soviet industry, including the quarterly, half-yearly, and annual statistical reports on the fulfillment of the National Plan.[29] There was also other evidence of dogmatic resistance. In October 1966 *Pravda* castigated unnamed "local party and economic leaders" who "deliberately obstruct the implementation of the new system." "In other words," wrote *Pravda*, "they support the reform, but so far they have taken no serious organizational and technical measures for its practical implementation" (220, p. 1).

But despite this rear-guard resistance and deliberate obstruction by conservative elements, the new system was spreading. By the end of 1966, 673 industrial enterprises, employing more than two million workers, as well as two sections of the national railway network and an undisclosed number of road, river, maritime, and air transportation enterprises and trade undertakings, were switched to the new system (221, p. 9).[30] Evaluating the progress of these experimental enterprises, *Pravda* hastened to add the in-

---

[29] For instance in the statistical report on the fulfillment of the National Plan in 1966, published in *Pravda* (January 29, 1967), in which the performance of experimental enterprises was singled out for particular praise. Also the Soviet Planning Chief Nikolai Baibakov, in an interview in *Pravda* (November 4, 1966), said that preliminary results "show convincingly the great opportunities the new system of planning and economic incentives opens for higher efficiency of production."

[30] N.B.: According to *Pravda* (February 16, 1967), the number of enterprises which switched over to the new system has increased to 2,200.

evitable formula that "practice has shown that the economic reform produces perceptible positive results." At the same time the Soviet protagonists of economic pragmatism were trying to convince their opponents that there is no contradiction between decentralization of economic decision-making and the basic principles of "socialist planned economy." One example here is an article published in the Bulletin of the Soviet Academy of Sciences by L. V. Kantorovich (213). Urging the more widespread use of mathematical methods to achieve optimal planning, Kantorovich argued that:

> The system of optimal planning in no way presupposes the full centralization of economic decisions. On the contrary, because the optimal economic plan can be combined with a coordinated system of prices and other social evaluations (the rate of return of capital, land rent, rent for raw materials . . . , etc.), it is possible for decisions to be taken locally which are coordinated to the maximum extent with the interests of the national economy. This contributes to the widespread utilization of the initiative of the production staffs, to the possibility of mobilizing local resources and discovering local reserves; it permits the expansion of the rights of individual economic sectors, and the build-up of a system of evaluation and stimulation of the work of these sectors, whereby that which is profitable for society as a whole also becomes profitable for each factory. In other words such a system creates the theoretical basis for solving the problem of combining centralized guidance of the economy with widespread local rights and initiative on the basis of economic methods of management. (213)

While the rest of the Soviet industry is scheduled to be switched to the new system of management by 1968, other economic reforms are also in the offing. One of them is a wholesale price reform which is to take place gradually throughout 1967. The broad principles of this reform were explained and its timetable outlined in detail by V. Sitnin, the Chairman of the Soviet State Prices Committee, in a long article published in *Kommunist* (217). Sitnin repeats the slogan of the 23rd Congress concerning an overall reduction of retail prices, and argues that because of this it is not possible to raise wholesale prices so much that losses would result in the consumer industries. He criticizes one school of economists, which has argued for a sharper increase in wholesale prices on the theory that after the reform there should be only one price level for both group "A" and "B." Sitnin finds this view unrealistic, because in group "B" there are whole industries which are unprofitable (such as meat, milk, and fishing) coexisting with highly profitable industries such as wines, spirits, and tobacco.

In heavy industry the highly profitable oil and gas industries coexist with coal mining and iron ore extraction among the big losers. Sitnin claims that to overcome all these differences a 40–45 per cent increase in heavy industry prices would be needed, which is too big a leap for the immediate future.

For this reason the reform of wholesale prices will only partially reflect the need for profitability. The average increase is to be in the region of 11–12 per cent, giving a normal average profitability margin of 15 per cent in the working capital employed. The new wholesale prices for both heavy industry and group "B" will take effect on July 1, 1967. As from the beginning of 1967 new prices will be introduced in the light and food industries in order to make the transfer to the reformed system of management feasible.

Sitnin also makes it clear that the new wholesale prices are only an interim solution and that another overhaul of the price system can be expected before 1971 (when the next five-year plan is due to begin). But he ends his article by rejecting free price formation as an "idealized practice of the first years of the N.E.P." But he immediately qualifies this dogmatic statement on behalf of his own Committee's administrative rule by saying that:

> in the future we should more widely introduce the practice of fixing calculation norms *which allow the factories themselves to form prices on the basis of these norms, and should introduce limit prices. The time has come to increase the role and expand the rights of the factory in price formation. Evidently in the next year or two we shall gradually have to accumulate experience in this field*, to perfect the mechanism of price formation, on the essential condition of a single state price policy and of the guiding role of the state in price formation. (217) [italics added]

This may well mean that the Soviet policy makers would watch the flexible price experiments in other Moscow bloc countries and maybe try an experiment or two on their own. But essentially the Soviet Union, like Poland, evidently prefers to retain the price determination policy as the prerogative of central planners. And thus we have one more proof of its more cautious and more conservative approach to economic reforms.

In this respect the situation in Yugoslavia is certainly different. As far as economic pragmatism is concerned, Yugoslavia is not only far ahead of any Moscow bloc country, but in fact is playing the reformist game in quite a different league. While the other countries are still essentially trying to improve the old, traditional system of planning and management, the Yugoslavs are making a real effort to evolve a workable alternative—an altogether new system. For the others the basic question is what degree of decentralization and quasi-market economy is still compatible with central planning and party control. For the Yugoslavs the essential question seems to be how much central planning can be tolerated in an economic system geared to a relatively free market mechanism.

This comparison is not quite fair, since Yugoslavia is a decade or more ahead in its experience with economic reform. That experience has a rich literature of its own and does not really belong within the framework of this book, which is mainly concerned with various aspects of economic pragmatism in that part of the communist bloc which still remains (more or less) loyal to Moscow. However, a thumbnail sketch of the latest phase of Yugoslav reforms may well be in order, since, in a certain sense it provides a preview of what may happen in Eastern Europe in the next five years or so should the rapid progress of economic pragmatism continue at its present pace.

In this respect the economic reforms embarked upon by Belgrade at the end of July 1965 (242, pp. 1–4, 252) are a real milestone, not only for Yugoslavia itself, but perhaps for all other communist countries as well. If we discount the workers' council aspect of those reforms as a specific Titoist phenomenon, what is now happening in Yugoslavia gives us a glimpse at the future course of the reformist approach in Eastern Europe. For in the early sixties Yugoslavia went through the inevitable phase of the bitter struggle between the opponents of economic reforms and the defenders of centralized control on one side and the protagonists of realistic economic approach on the other. This struggle has now reached the stage at which some of the more extremist advocates of the new economic system claim that not only the state but the party as well no longer has any place in running economic affairs (248).

True, neither Tito nor his close lieutenants share this view. But the fact remains that the net effect of the July 1965 reforms must be the gradual reduction of the role of central planners and of the party hierarchy. Even before the latest reform, many leading personalities of the Titoist regime, such as Valdimir Bakaric, were openly advocating a change-over to a full market economy (230). But the actual reforms fell short of this.

The way for the July reforms had been prepared at the Eighth Party Congress held in Belgrade in the first half of December 1964. All the major weaknesses of the Yugoslav economy were openly discussed and corrective measures adopted. The final resolution expressly condemned "administrative control exercised by political factors," and called for "a freer play of the market mechanism" and the "abolition of price regulation by administrative measures" (247).

In the light of these sweeping statements the July reforms came almost as an anticlimax because they seemed to be mainly fiscal and technocratic, rather than ideological and declarative. But it is precisely such concrete measures, rather than high-sounding declarations of principles, that are necessary to break the back of centralized state control. The essence of the July 1965 reforms was an increase in the direct control of producers over manufacture and distribution, and the gradual withdrawal of central state institutions from economic decision-making.

One basic reform, for instance, permits the enterprise to retain 71 per cent of its net profits, as compared with the 51 per cent allowed previously. Consequently the share surrendered to the state dropped to 29 per cent as against its former 49 per cent (243). This means that the bulk of available operational and investment funds remains at the enterprise level, subject to local decision as to its use. The share of the state can henceforth be regarded as a form of profit tax, rather than a transfer of investment funds to the use of central planners.

A drastic reduction in state subsidies to the less efficient enterprises is also likely to have far-reaching effects. On the one hand it should promote competition on the domestic market, leading to the gradual elimination of less efficient producers; on the other it must spur a drive toward real profitability, making the producers both cost and market conscious.

Finally, the price determination system was drastically overhauled and the price-fixing prerogatives of the central planners were radically reduced, with strict price control retained only for basic necessities.[31]

The short-term effects of all these liberalizing measures coupled with a drastic devaluation of the dinar were adverse.[32] Prices began to soar (as much from higher import costs as from scarcities). The government was forced to step in with some *ad hoc* restrictive measures. There were also mass dismissals of unneeded workers, the inevitable effect of the drive for greater profitability. But by mid-October 1965, the inflation curve had begun to flatten out and the amount of money in circulation was said to be only four per cent higher than a year before (239).

Unemployment nevertheless continued to increase and the Yugoslav authorities gave their official blessing to labor migration to the West (236, 244). Despite a substantial rise in average earnings, the standard of living declined. All those short-term negative effects have their roots in the initial imbalance of the Yugoslav economy, but they show the difficulties which the other countries must face as they follow the road of reform.[33]

Such difficulties are the price which will have to be paid for the rationalization of the communist economic system. There is no magic formula which, in the space of few months, can radically cure an economic organism ruined by long years of central planning. An initial period of great difficulties and substantial belt-tightening is inevitable, and this is bound to provide ammunition for the opponents of reform. However, since there is no realistic alternative, the Yugoslav experience is an indication of the problems which other communist countries will be facing in the not too distant future.

---

31 As the prices skyrocketed following the reform, price controls were temporarily reimposed. But a law providing for a return to free market prices was approved by the Yugoslav Parliament in March 1967.

32 From 750 Dinars to 1250 per dollar.

33 These problems are discussed in more detail in Chapter 7.

4

★

PRICES AND MARKET ECONOMY

Of all the various aspects of economic reforms, the issue of prices is certainly the most crucial and, at the same time, the most controversial. There are three main problems involved here: Who should fix the prices? How are the prices to be determined and by whom? And what function should the price have in a reformed, but still Marxist, planned economy? It is no exaggeration to say that the way in which these three problems are ultimately resolved may well determine the success or failure of all the economic reforms which are now being introduced throughout Eastern Europe.

Ostensibly, the solution seems obvious. A return to a quasi-market economy is the avowed long-term aim of all the pragmatist measures. And—to quote a Czech Marxist economist—"The system of management, based on the use of market mechanism, requires that prices should be determined in accordance with the market conditions, and should not be the result of more or less subjective decisions, as used to be the rule in the past" (39). In other words, prices should be determined by the interplay of supply and demand.

There are also other compelling reasons for adopting at least a limited free prices system. The primary one is, of course, the acceptance of profit as the mainspring of all economic activity, and the discarding of the traditional basic measuring rod of communist planning—the value of global output. Some of the Marxist economists would like to argue that this change-over concerns nothing more than the practices of economic planning and the techniques of management. The proposed new measures, they claim, would consist of replacing the hitherto basic indicator, that is, the value of global production, by the concept of profit (155). Such a substitution, in itself, is supposed to provide a magic cure for all the main shortcomings of the traditional economic system. But will it? And are we really dealing here only with the methods of planning and the technique of management?

In seeking an answer to these questions, let us consider what are the probable long-term effects of replacing the indicator of global production by that of profit. One could argue that over a period of time the principle of the profit motive must lead eventually to a fundamental change, as far as the real goals of all economic activity are concerned. For what were the practical effects of the old supreme measuring rod? In essence, they boiled down to the fact that all the productive efforts at the factory level were directed toward achieving the highest possible value of the annual output, regardless not only of potential demand, but quite often regardless of the specific production directives issued by the central planners. This global value was, after all, the basic criterion for assessing the performance of any socialized enterprise (51).

This has inevitably led to many anomalies. More expensive goods were produced in preference to cheaper ones, in clear defiance of market requirements. Technical inmprovements were postponed in order not to hold back the smooth flow of mass produced output. In short, production was carried out for production's sake alone. The net result was an ever-growing disparity between the actual output and the effective demand—both the consumer demand and the industrial requirements. The managers of individual factories had but one goal. To produce as many goods as possible, regardless of the actual cost of doing so and, worse still, regardless of the fact of whether there was any demand for the goods they produced.

It is, of course, hard to believe that the introduction of the profit motive would change, from one day to another, the psychological attitude of the managers of the socialized enterprises, and even the keenest protagonists of the reform are well aware of this (47). For the concept of profit encompasses not only actual production of goods, but also their sale. Such an interpretation of the meaning of profit, and there cannot be any other one, introduces a direct connection between profile of output, effective demand, and prices. In other words, a producer who is guided by the profit motive must pay close attention to the needs of the market.

In this way, at least as far as consumer goods are concerned, the acceptance of the measuring rod of profitability inevitably leads to the next logical step—the recognition of the principle of the sovereignty of the consumer. And from here it is not very far to the adoption of at least some aspects of market economy. This is confirmed by the tendencies evident in the rapid change-over of the Yugoslav economic system in the last few months and by the trend discernible in the Czechoslovak, East German, Hungarian, Polish, and Bulgarian reforms.

But one must have no illusions that the acceptance of the profit motive will, by itself, logically lead to the return to a market economy. The problem here is not only one of unavoidable resistance of dogmatic elements, but also a more important question of objective difficulties. In short, the profit motive cannot be fully meaningful within the framework of a system of arbitrarily set wages and prices.

It is for this very reason that the more extremist economic reformers in Eastern Europe argue that both wages and prices must be set completely free, to find their own level through the interplay of supply and demand (6). This may seem a logical and straightforward solution, but in the specific economic conditions which prevail in the communist part of Europe the problem is not as simple as it sounds.

First of all, one has to accept the fact that an entirely free price system, determined exclusively by supply and demand, does not exist anywhere in the world, outside those chapters of economic textbooks which deal with the theories of the classics of laissez-faire. Even in a normal market economy, price determination is subject to several outside factors of a more or less subjective nature. Many producers take every opportunity to charge "what the traffic would bear," while governments often intervene either to slap a sales tax on the producer's own price or, alternatively, to keep the prices down. One may well recall here the pressures applied by the U.S. government in respect to aluminum and steel prices, as well as the British price and wage freeze.

All these external factors stem from the fact that market mechanism can no longer be regarded as the sole and infallible regulator of prices. In a modern industrial society, highly conscious of the need for a greater degree of social justice and economic stability, other factors have to be taken into account. National economic interest, monetary equilibrium, preservation of minimum living standards, or balance of payment problems are only some of the generally accepted reasons for subjective factors of certain selected prices, or price groups, regardless of market mechanism.

The same motives for state intervention apply, of course, to any price system which may eventually evolve in the individual countries of Eastern Europe. But in addition there are others, peculiar to communist economies, which as a rule are far more vulnerable to the vagaries of a free price system. For one thing, there are just too many enterprises there which enjoy a monopolistic position in their particular line of output (49). This is the heritage of the era of "gigantomania" and industrial concentration. Secondly, all the countries of Eastern Europe are notoriously short of foreign currencies. And thus, they are hardly in a position to attempt to restore market equilibrium in respect to any category of goods by appropriate imports—even if the governments in question were ever inclined to pursue such policy.[1]

But the main reason why an entirely free price system cannot be introduced, even in respect to the consumer goods, at least in the short run, are the gaping shortages on the supply side. The situation in East Europe today is not unlike that of the West during and immediately after the war. There are simply not enough consumer goods to go around. This is not necessarily true of all the goods, but there are enough products in short supply to make the more responsible economic reformers shudder about the possible short-term effects of adopting an unrestricted market mechanism.[2] More so, since the existing industrial potential in most of the countries of Eastern Europe cannot be expected to catch

[1] The Yugoslav government does seem inclined to use imports as the weapon to combat the excessive price increases on the part of home producers (see 249).

[2] For instance, Sik argues vehemently that under existing supply conditions there is a danger of a "speculative price boost by the enterprises, especially those which are in a monopolistic position" (49).

up with the domestic demand for several years to come, even if a consumer-oriented economy were to become a reality.

On top of that there is the problem of the hidden excess of purchasing power, the sudden release of which would tend to produce a dangerous inflationary spiral. Years of acute shortages of high quality consumer goods and the practical impossibility of any significant private investment in such areas as housing and other forms of property are largely responsible for heavily swollen saving accounts in all the more industrialized countries of Eastern Europe. This is a symptom of suppressed inflation, which may well be released if price controls were to be removed. Many East European economists are well aware of this potential danger.[3] They know that those are not normal savings, but an unrealized purchasing power. Money which would be thrown on the market, as soon as some more attractive consumer goods made their appearance. And since the shortages would, no doubt, persist, the prices are bound to rocket upward.

How serious this problem really is can be easily seen from Table 1, which compares the growth rate of personal savings with that of real wages in the case of the Soviet Union.

The situation in other Moscow bloc countries is very similar

TABLE *1.*

Year	*Savings*[4] *(mill. rubles)*	*Growth* *Absolute (mill. rubles)*	*Percentage*	*Percentage growth of real wages*[5]
1958	8719	661	8.2	3
1959	10056	1337	15.3	3
1960	10909	853	8.5	4
1961	11671	762	7.0	4
1962	12745	1074	9.2	4
1963	13992	1247	9.8	4
1964	15707	1715	12.3	4
1965	18727	3020	19.2	4
1966	22900	4173	22.0	6 (estimate)

[3] Cf. the speech of Vaclav Skoda in the Czechoslovak National Assembly, *Rude Pravo*, December 16, 1965.

[4] Source, *National Economy of USSR in 1965* (Moscow, 1966).

[5] Interpolated from *National Economy of USSR in 1965*, p. 593—real wages rose between 1958 and 1965 by 30 per cent.

and the dynamics of growth of personal savings of anything are comparably even higher in relation to per capita income.

Of course the problem of unrealized purchasing power is of the regime's own making. It is mainly due to past policies of devoting a large proportion of national income to investment purposes, with an emphasis on heavy industry. But there were other contributing factors which stem not so much from a dogmatic approach to the needs of consumption but from the malfunctioning of the system itself. The ever-growing length of the investment cycle tied up productive resources without adding anything to the manufacturing capacity. The perennial disparity between actual output and effective demand resulted in ever-rising stocks of unsold consumer goods. But regardless of past and present errors of economic policy, the fact remains that the inflationary dangers inherent in the problem of unrealized purchasing power undoubtedly make it more difficult to adopt a free price system.

All these specific conditions prevailing in Eastern Europe recommend great caution in tackling the price reform. It would be obviously foolhardy to remove all price controls at once. But that should be no excuse for keeping all price controls indefinitely, or worse, for retaining direct price control as a principle. Gradual removal of restrictions and the greatest degree of flexibility seem to be the only rational way out (58).

Not all the countries of Eastern Europe have opted for this sensible solution. By now we have a pretty definite picture of the apparent intentions of the individual East European regimes regarding a new price system and the extent to which they are willing to accept the market mechanism as the instrument of price determination.

Broadly speaking, two different groups have emerged. One, composed of Poland and the Soviet Union, has apparently opted for the indefinite retention of price fixing by central authority. The other, i.e., Czechoslovakia, Hungary, Bulgaria, and to some extent East Germany, seem to be willing to try some significant experiments to give the market mechanism a chance to prove its worth. Two countries defy classification at the moment. The Rumanians, true to their style, are playing their economic reform cards so close to their chest that it is impossible to say what they have in mind, and the Yugoslavs who are ahead of all the Moscow bloc countries and play the reformist game in quite another league. Yugoslavia appears now to be heading toward a full market economy in which a free price system is just a question of time.[6]

The worst thing about the Polish and Soviet approach to the issue of price determination is not that these countries seem inclined to retain the system of centrally fixed prices for the time being, but that so far they have shown no signs of being prepared to abandon this principle in any foreseeable future. As far as Poland is concerned, the party authorities there went as far as to state explicitly that even the retail prices of those goods which are in plentiful supply should be centrally controlled. "In no case," said the Polish Chief Planner Jedrychowski in his keynote speech at the July 1965 Party Plenum, which approved the blueprint for economic reforms up until 1970, "can we agree to a free movement of prices uncontrolled by the state, or to a spontaneous shaping of prices . . . by supply and demand" (193).

No switch-over to a more flexible price system can be expected in the Soviet Union either. Although Kosygin in his speech at the September 1965 Party Plenum was not as emphatic on this subject as the Poles, he nevertheless made it quite clear that the principle of price control will be retained (223). V. Sitnin, the Chairman of the newly organized state Committee for Prices, discussing later the role of prices as an instrument of economic policy was far more specific (216). It appears that the Russians intend to adopt a system of centrally fixed prices, which will be periodically revised in the light of market conditions. And while all prices, including the retail ones, will be in fact fixed by the central planners, there would exist a possibility for more efficient manufacturers to charge less for their products than the official state price (they will not, however, be permitted to charge more). This small escape clause may have some effect on certain supply prices, especially of semi-finished products where a direct supplier-consumer relationship does exist. One can hardly expect, however, that such voluntary price reductions would be applied to consumer goods, unless in a very limited category of hard sale products and certainly not in a sellers' market type of economy

---

[6] Despite the temporary reintroduction of price controls following the inflationary trend after the July 1965 reforms.

where the volume of profits is to be the basis for determining bonuses paid both to the managers and to the workers. It seems much more likely that the maximum prices, as fixed by the State Committee for Prices, would be normally charged throughout the Soviet Union.

The situation in East Germany is less clear. Until the very end of 1965, it seemed pretty obvious that the Ulbricht regime would like to contain most of its economic reforms within the realm of decentralization limited to the framework of the eighty odd VVB's, while keeping the prerogatives of price determination in the hands of central planners (93). But in the keynote speech which Ulbricht made at the December 1965 Plenum of the SED Control Committee, he seemed to indicate that a more flexible approach to the issue of prices will be adopted in East Germany. According to him, the forthcoming third stage of the supply prices reform would create a new situation:

> This new phase of price policy requires a great flexibility of price determination within industry. The point is to systematically adapt the prices to the values and to take into consideration the changing conditions and claims of the market. Thereby the prices will exert a real stimulating effect on the increase of economic efficiency. These new prices will be flexible; they will follow the socially necessary expenditures for production. (92)

This new official line on the issue of price determination was followed by an article contributed for discussion in *Einheit*, the party's periodical for theoretical questions, in which flexibility of prices was again advocated (87).

A full-fledged conference on the role of the market system was held in the first half of March 1966 during which the "second phase of the new economic system was vividly discussed."[7] According to the official report on this meeting:

> A major subject was the role of the market in the socialist planned economy. . . . The socialist economy considers the market an important phase of the production process.

In his speech to the East German 21st People's Chamber Session on September 1, 1966, Finance Minister Willy Rumpf dealt ex-

---

[7] *Neues Deutschland* (March 15, 1966).

tensively with the forthcoming third stage in the supply prices reform and its effects. About the same time a highly significant article by Kurt Ambree and Helmut Mann appeared in *Einheit* on variable prices (88).

In his keynote speech at the September 1966 Control Committee Plenum, Politburo member G. Mittag noted that "the system of comprehensive price control as an important aspect of implementing the second phase of the new economic system and developing the over-all system of control has not yet been drafted."[8] He concluded, however, that

> It is now essential in industrial price control to establish a proper link between administrative control exercised by central price sections and the economic methods of price control, for example, through the influence exerted by primary customers on the price level and in compliance with price regulations, as well as through the influence exerted by the end producers on supplies and so forth.

Anticipating the forthcoming third stage in price reform, the East German official gazette published an order establishing new constant plan prices in 1967, which are to be effective for evaluating industrial production on January 1, 1968.[9] These new prices were meant to replace the fixed plan prices introduced in 1955.[10]

While all this sounded rather confusing, a much better insight into the longer-term intentions of the Ulbricht regime in respect to price-determination policy was provided by an important article on this subject published by an East German economist in the Soviet periodical *Ekonomicheska Gazieta* (89, p. 39). The author, Dr. M. Bettherr, advocated the adoption of four types of prices: a) "fixed," b) "maximum," c) "calculated" (established by the enterprise on the basis of instructions and in cooperation with

---

[8] Mittag's keynote speech as published in *Neues Deutschland* (September 18, 1966).

[9] Order issued September 9, 1966 and published in *Gesetzblatt der Deutschen Demokratischen Republik* (October 25, 1966).

[10] According to Mittag, the new price base will alter the figures used to measure past economic performance. Thus for 1965, as a result of the new measuring rod, the total social production will increase by about 19 billion marks to 200 billion; production consumption will increase by about 23 billion marks to 117 billion, and produced national income will decrease by about 4 billion, down to 83 billion. These new valuations, of course, in no way change the physical output.

price-determining agencies), and d) "contract" (determined by the buyer and seller). This was the first definite indication that a multiple price system was being considered for the East German economic model.

There is little doubt that the 1967 reform of supply prices means the beginning of a period of increased economic significance of prices. Three years of experience with a more rigid price determination system has apparently led East Germany to recognize the need for the introduction of a more functional price system. In their already mentioned article in *Einheit,* Ambree and Mann summarized the reasons for a flexible method of price determination as part of the system of economic levers (88).

They recognized that one cannot have periodic price reforms and expect continuity of price formation. The problem is in particular made more acute by the rapid changes in production which can be expected in the future and the need for a quick response of prices to these changes. All that central price authorities could do, according to Ambree and Mann, is to engage in long-term price planning. These price fixing agencies can only provide the basic price orientation and should not be engaged in the determination of individual prices.

This change in the function of the central price authorities requires a devolution of price-making powers to the VVB's and the economic ministries. As Ambree and Mann put it:

> An important task for the new phase of price policy in the second stage of the new economic system lies, furthermore, in the determination of the responsibility of the other state organs for the formation of prices and to prepare the VVB's for the taking over of its new functions.
>
> In this connection it has to be investigated to what extent the right to regulate prices for certain goods and commodity groups can be transferred to the VVB's and the ministries. (88)

In whatever way the price determination system in East Germany would eventually evolve (and one simply does not know how much official backing is behind Dr. Bettherr's "four price types" proposal), the degree of centralized control is likely to be greater than in Czechoslovakia, Hungary, and perhaps even in Bulgaria.

The same is true to a still greater extent in respect to those countries, like Poland and the Soviet Union, which so far insist on retaining the principle that all prices are to be fixed by the central authorities. This does not mean that the pricing policy will remain the same as it was in the Stalin era. Far from it. The old cost-plus method of arbitrary price fixing will definitely be abandoned. Raw material and semi-finished goods prices, as well as the cost of energy will be brought much nearer to their true economic level. And this would permit a much more realistic formula for determining prices to evolve. But the basic principle of state control of all retail prices is likely to be retained. And this, regardless of all differences in the actual choice of the price fixing techniques, sets the Soviet Union and Poland (and of course Rumania) as a group apart, at least for the time being.

The other group is composed of Czechoslovakia, Hungary, and Bulgaria, which have opted for a different solution of the price determination dilemma: a three-category pricing system. However, since the final shape of the Bulgarian economic reform is still not quite certain (although the principle of price determination has already been made clear)[11] it may be best to leave it out of our analysis for the time being and concentrate on the measures proposed in Prague and Budapest.

The essence of the Czech and Hungarian reforms is a significant break with the principles of arbitrary directives from above and full state control. These twin pillars of economic dogmatism are to be replaced within the framework of forthcoming reforms by more flexible indirect controls. Thus the Czechs and the Hungarians have been able to free themselves more fully from their dogmatic heritage, as well as from the pressure of the economic vested interests. In carrying out their reform they did not follow the past of sheer opportunism and of taking into account the established priorities, but the road of rationalization and common sense.

One example of this common sense attitude is certainly a more pragmatic approach to the whole problem of price determination. The Czechoslovak and Hungarian economic reformers are as keenly aware as are their counterparts in the other Soviet bloc countries,

[11] See the section on Bulgarian economic reforms in Chapter 3.

of the dangerous pitfalls inherent in switching over to a free price system all at once (49). The supply position in respect to the great majority of consumer goods is such that should free prices be introduced, the market mechanism would inevitably break down. But there are certain categories of products, where the market equilibrium is clearly within reach. And this fact has been accepted as one of the decisive factors in the more rational approach to the problem of price determination. Thus the most essential characteristic of the Czech and Hungarian proposals for a reform of the price system is that the starting point is not an abstract principle, but the realities of the supply and demand position (99).

This pragmatic approach to the problem of prices is fully consistent with the basic assumption of the Czech and Hungarian reforms, namely that even in a communist type of planned economy, individual enterprise must base its activity on full economic cost accounting. And this concept is understood here in a much broader sense than elsewhere in the bloc. Instead of a complicated method of promoting the operation of the profit motive and the still more complex way of computing the profits and the premiums, a very simple principle is to be the mainspring of the Czechoslovak and Hungarian reforms. Each enterprise must earn enough to pay its expenses; earn—by selling the article which it produces (51).

This type of approach created the necessary logical link between the planned-for output, the price and the effective demand, a link based on the strongest of all human motives: economic self-interest. Obviously, however, such a relationship is only possible provided there is some hope of achieving a reasonable market equilibrium, without eliminating just the marginal buyers, or where the supply already exceeds demand. Otherwise an inflationary spiral is bound to be touched off. And the inflation bogey is, indeed (apart from the dogmatic resistance) the main braking force holding down the impetus of economic revisionism on the sector of prices (and wages).

Once those basic considerations are accepted, it becomes quite obvious that one cannot approach the problem of price determination in a highly vulnerable economy in a uniform manner. Apart from the supply and demand position, there are certain categories of goods in which an increase in prices would inevitably set in motion significant inflationary pressures throughout the wh[illegible] economy, and others in which such a rise would have only a limited local effect. There are products a price hike of which could be politically explosive, and others where it is politically neutral, except for harmless grumbling (37). All this, looking at things from the point of view of the party authorities, calls for a great deal of political acumen, for extreme caution, and for a certain dose of sophisticated pragmatism in all attempts to reform the pricing system.

One way to satisfy all these requirements is to adopt different methods of price determination for specific groups of products, giving more leeway to the market mechanism in the case of those goods where the supply-demand position is better and retaining control of prices of potential inflation starters and politically sensitive products (23). This is, of course, a rule of thumb method, nevertheless it is more selective and pragmatic than the principle of indiscriminate price fixing. Such an approach has evidently won the way in Czechoslovakia, Hungary, and (seemingly) Bulgaria.

The result is a three-category price system, envisaged in the blueprints for economic reform in all three countries. There are some minor differences in details which stem mainly from diverging economic realities. But the underlying principle is the same in all three cases. All products are to be divided into three basic groups and for each category another method (not to say principle) of price determination has been proposed. Such division defines also the prerogatives of both the immediate producers and of the central planners in respect to price determination (51).

Both the rationale behind this more pragmatic approach and its practical implementation are best and the most authoritatively documented so far in the case of Czechoslovakia. Here, as in Hungary and Bulgaria, there will be three different categories of prices: fixed, flexible (or limited movement prices) and free (57). Fixed prices will be fully controlled by the central planners and any change proposed by the immediate producers would require a decision of the central price-fixing authority. Flexible prices will be set free either within the range of upper and lower limits, or alternatively with only the maximum price ceiling—both set by the central planners. This means that the market mechanism could operate only within the price range decreed by Prague and that its the producers will be free to charge any price, ie effective demand, would permit them to maxi- ts. Finally, the free prices will be permitted to find as in a normal market economy. In this category, of price determination would devolve entirely to nediate producers.

egory system of prices is certainly more pragmatic and gives more elbow room to maneuver than the more dogmatic approach of indiscriminate price control. But how far does it lead along the road toward a market economy? To answer this one must know what types of goods have been assigned to each category and what ratio of the overall volume of all products has been assigned to each of them. Or, to put it more simply, how significant are the concessions to market mechanism in terms of global turnover on the macro-economic scale.

Here again the only concrete data are available for Czechoslovakia. It appears that in this country, at least in the initial stage, roughly two thirds (actually 64 per cent) of the total volume of output will still be subject to strict price control, while for more than one third (36 per cent) the prices will be determined partly or wholly by the interplay of supply and demand. But the situation is actually less rosy than it would appear from these percentages. In terms of global output, only 7 per cent of all the products would fall into the free price category, 14.7 per cent would be subject to a maximum price restraint and 14.3 per cent will be permitted to fluctuate within the upper and lower limits set by the central planners.

If one takes the consumer goods alone, the situation does not look much better. Here the proposed ratio is as follows: fixed prices, 78 per cent; flexible prices, 11 per cent; and free prices, 11 per cent (57). Looking at the problem from another angle, one ought to note that all basic raw materials and nearly all foodstuffs (92 per cent) have been included in the fixed price category. So, in actual fact, the operation of the market mechanism has been limited only to some semi-finished products and selected manufactured consumer goods, with the bulk of them still subjected to some limitation of free movement of prices.

Still it is only a beginning. And once one has accepted the assumption that the change in the pricing system must be gradual, the final judgment ought to be suspended until one can see cle what further steps would follow. The crucial question is one of th dynamics of movement within the three price types. Would the free price category gradually expand at the expense of the two other groups? Would the preponderance of fixed prices be gradually undermined? It is too early, as yet, to give an analytically sound answer to those questions. The pioneering Czechoslovak scheme is still in its initial experimental stage. The precise lines of the Hungarian economic reform are not yet definitely drawn, while the Bulgarian blueprint is still nothing more than a purely theoretical proposal.

The sheer logic of the three-category system would seem to imply that products would be moved to a more liberal pricing group as soon as the supplies have sufficiently improved in relation to the potential demand, and this certainly seems to be the intention of the Czechoslovak regime (37). If there is no objective reason to fear a significant price increase, this rule could also be applied to politically sensitive products (such as food and clothing) and to less essential raw materials. The whole trend of official economic thinking behind the new approach to price value theory seems to be pointing in that direction (23). But under the communist system the trend of official thinking can easily be reversed by ideological imponderables and the logical way is not necessarily the obvious one.

There are also many other important factors which ought to be pointed out here. First of all, there is the public attitude on the problem of price reform. To an average Westerner, born and bred in the conditions of a market economy, the advantages of a free price system seem nearly beyond discussion. He naturally, not to say automatically, associates price fixing and the principle of governmental control over demand with wartime scarcities.

After twenty odd years of experiencing the communist type of planned economy, the attitude of an average East European is different. He has a deep-rooted suspicion of any price reform, since all previous readjustment of prices invariably left him worse off than he was before. This accounts for the fact that, whatever the learned economists and reformers may think, the average Czech and Hungarian worker regards the introduction of a three-category price system as, at best, a mixed blessing (see 59, 110).

note the fact that the first public reaction in disclosure of a new price determination system ding rumors of a price increase."[12] So much so n party leaders detailed Politburo member Jeno official denial, which, incidentally, a few weeks be untrue.[13] Indeed, the Hungarian regime com- litical error of increasing the prices of certain essentials, consumer goods, services, and the cost of social security contributions, before even taking the first concrete steps toward an economic reform.

In the light of such experiences one should not be surprised that the average East European has a deep-rooted suspicion that the introduction of even a limited free price system is just a handy excuse for an increase in prices. The basic reason for that is the rather one-sided approach of the people in authority to the market mechanism. The trend toward a free movement of prices is not matched by any inclination to increase the wage rates (24).[14]

Indeed no known blueprint of economic reform in Eastern Europe envisages any real compensation in the form of higher wage rates to offset the inevitable price increases. Only the early version of the Polish economic model (long since abandoned) put the reform of wages and prices on equal footing (188). In all other known schemes underpaid labor is apparently to remain the main source of communist capital accumulation. At the same time the fear remains that state control would not be a full-proof guarantee against arbitrary price increases (24).

This explains the divergence of public attitudes on the issue of free prices as far as Western and Eastern Europe is concerned. Here and there the trend of prices is upward, although until now this trend has been more marked in Western Europe. But the average Western worker is not really apprehensive about the mild inflationary tendencies of the price level and accepts them as natural phenomena. He knows from experience that his earnings will continue to grow at a still higher rate. In the conditions of labor shortage, it is easy for the trade unions to keep up the dif-

---

12 *Nepszabadsag*, November 30, 1965.

13 *Nepszabadsag* (December 19, 1965).

14 See also "ir," "The Relationship of Wages and the Cost of Living," *Zemledelske Noviny* (December 23, 1966).

ferential. The worker in Eastern Europe completely lacks this feeling of financial security. He has no hope that his earnings will keep pace with prices, once the upward trend of prices becomes really marked.

The whole subject of short-term negative effects of economic reforms, of which price increases are but one aspect, is a very intricate one and they will be discussed at length in Chapter 7. It had to be mentioned briefly, however, to explain why the reform of prices along the lines of even limited market mechanism has not received such widespread public support throughout Eastern Europe as an average Westerner would naturally expect.

The issue of public support, however, or the widespread fear of price increases, for that matter, are not the decisive influence as far as the decisions made by party authorities are concerned. In any case, the public attitude on the issue of economic pragmatism remains contradictory. A powerful pressure (mainly exerted by the intellectuals and economists, although it has a wider popular backing) toward the rationalization of the economic system undoubtedly exists. So does the apprehension about the immediate short-term effects of the necessary reforms. But the overwhelming factor remains the manifest failure of the traditional system of planning and managing the national economy and the consequent economic stagnation. Basically it is a question of adapting the structure of the supply to effective demand and introducing the proper relationship between the true economic cost and the final price. In this respect, the communist regimes in Eastern Europe have no other alternative. The only way to the eventual rationalization of their economies leads through a reform of the price system.

The first stage of such a reform must be the adjustment of supply (industrial) and wholesale prices. Otherwise any attempt to introduce a proper relationship between the cost and the selling price, as well as the adoption of a market mechanism would have no real economic meaning.

Recognizing the basic need for such a reform, most of the countries of Eastern Europe have already begun to bring their supply prices nearer to their true economic level. In East Germany the third stage of the reform of supply prices is scheduled for

1967.[15] Poland, after a rather fragmentary supply price reform in the late fifties, and again in 1960, is to carry out the next installment of such reform during 1967–68 (see 183). Czechoslovakia and Hungary plan a complete overhaul of their wholesale and supply prices by 1968 (21, 38, 99). There is, however, one significant difference between the Polish and East German reforms and the Czechoslovak and Hungarian ones. While the two former countries have in essence retained the function of fixing the supply prices as the prerogative of the central planners, the new Czechoslovak system of supply prices is intended to be more flexible and to reflect both the actual cost of production, as well as the world market prices (58, 60).

One has to recognize that in the conditions of a communist planned economy, the problem of supply prices is even more complex than that of retail prices. It involves the cost of basic raw materials, energy, investment goods, and semi-finished products. The question of what one state enterprise should charge another for, say, coal, machine tools, or bricks baffled communist economic thinkers from the very beginning. Some Marxist-Leninist purists argued even that there should be no charge whatsoever, since such a delivery meant merely a transfer of state (or all-nation) property from one place to another. This "free good" principle was still retained in respect to investment goods until very recently (46, 154). As for the other supply prices, they were fixed at an artificially low level by purely arbitrary decisions. Needless to say this was one of the basic reasons for a notorious and widespread waste of industrial resources (47).

The artificially low supply prices did not matter much in Stalin's era of a war-type economy when the real cost of production was, for all practical purposes, disregarded. But it became a most serious problem once the decision was taken to switch over to the principle of profitability. Clearly all those factories which worked primarily for the industrial enterprises could not ever hope to show a profit as long as they continued to deliver their products at near give-away prices (38). Nor was there any hope of ever establishing a sound cost-price relationship throughout the econ-

[15] As discussed above in the section on the East German pricing system.

omy as a whole, if the supply prices remained artificially low (see 99).

The obvious answer seemed to be to increase those prices to their true economic level, either through the cost-plus principle (i.e., the average production cost of, say, all coal mines plus an agreed margin of profit) or by bringing them up to the world market level (8, 30). With a judicious application of state-financed subsidies this could be done without eliminating marginal producers. But then the central planners would be faced with another dilemma. The users of supply goods would be unable to afford to pay those quasi-economic prices, without a substantial increase of the sale prices of their own products (37, 59). And such an increase, in turn, could not be carried out without a substantial increase in wages and salaries, since it was eventually bound to end with a general rise of all retail prices—in other words, the classic makings of an inflationary spiral.

Of course, the state could well absorb the bulk of all these price increases through a huge reduction of its sales tax (or the money which accrues to the state because of the difference between factory prices plus normal distribution costs and the final selling price). But, if this solution were to be adopted, the main source of capital accumulation and the basic means of financing all new investment would be dissipated at the enterprise level and would be removed out of the direct jurisdiction of central planners, unless an adequate levy on both circulating and fixed capital of individual factories would be introduced (60).

This is the basic reason for the cautious and gradual approach to the issue of reforming the supply price system which is generally regarded as a "long-term problem" (37). What most of the East European countries have in mind is simply a patchwork method of higher supply prices supplemented by a judicious use of hidden and overt subsidies to offset their full effect on the more sensitive sectors of economy (38, 86). The whole procedure, moreover, is to be subjected to the practice of price fixing by central planners and strict bureaucratic control.[16]

One small exception to this rule (as far as it is known) is

[16] At least in the case of Polish, Soviet, and East German reforms as demonstrated above in this chapter.

Czechoslovakia (and perhaps Hungary). What Prague apparently has in mind is some extension of its three-category method of price determination to be applied to selected supply prices. Under the forthcoming reform of the price system, the supply and wholesale prices, with the exception of agricultural purchasing prices and the transport charges, are to be divided into the same three groupings as outlined earlier in this chapter. It seems clear, however, at least from the now-available Czechoslovak material, that only a very limited quantity of the supply prices would be influenced by the market mechanism (23). As one of the official commentators put it:

> In view of the prevailing conditions in our economy, the maximal and minimal prices and the free prices will be for the time being applied only in the exceptional cases. Most prices will remain fixed or bound by the upper limit. . . . All kinds of raw materials, all kinds of fuel, all basic foundry, chemical and food products, basic building materials, hide, woods, etc., will be sold at fixed prices. (23)

Some flexibility is foreseen, however, for heavy engineering goods, assembly plants, and other manufactured supply products. Here the central planners would impose an upper price limit but a lower, mutually agreed, price can be settled bilaterally between the producer and the customer. The bulk of semi-finished products is apparently to be subject to this procedure. Clearly the final price here will be determined not only by the supply and demand position, but also by the respective monopolistic positions of the supplier and the customer.

All these measures can be expected to introduce only the marginal vestiges of market mechanism (38). Obviously, the communist regimes in Eastern Europe are not yet prepared to release the tight control over the whole sector of prices. They might be willing to make some marginal concessions for the sake of economic pragmatism, but not to the extent of accepting the inevitable implication of market economy, i.e., the principle of consumer sovereignty.

There is a valid reason for it, at least from the party leaders' point of view. The Czechoslovak premier, Lenart, for instance, did say publicly that "all levels of management, the makers of the plan and all producers must strictly respect the principle that all socialist efforts should be aimed at . . . the satisfaction of the consumer"(75), but no party leader worth his Marxist salt would apply this rule in actual practice without serious reservations. For once the consumer is allowed to decide what is going to be produced, the effective demand will not only determine the assortment of output of consumer goods, but in time, if allowed a free play, would inevitably begin to have a decisive influence on investment decisions. In due course, the consumer demand would actually determine the allocation of investment resources. And for this neither the mentality of party leaders in Eastern Europe nor the economic system itself are quite yet ready.

But the days of bureaucratic control and disdain for the market mechanism are numbered. As an eminent Polish economist put it:

> The negative attitude toward the market mechanism served quite well the socialist countries in their historic development. It was dressed up in a set of dogmatic prejudices, and during a given period, these dogmas were even quite useful. *But they are not useful now and have not been for quite some time.*
>
> At the present stage of our development, and this holds true for several other socialist countries, of basic importance is the exploitation of intensive growth factors, broader involvement of initiative and social activity, improving the rationality of action of all economic units, a better adjustment of production to needs, increasing the flexibility of action. All this is closely connected with the market mechanism. There seems to be no doubt today that the use of the market mechanism in the relations between various economic enterprises is especially closely associated with the task of introducing economic cost accounting and decentralization of management. Smooth and proper effect of the market mechanism is a precondition for the decentralization of management and for the proper functioning of economic cost accounting. (171, p. 164) [italics added]

And this brings us to the problem of decentralization, which will be discussed in the next chapter.

5

★

HOW MUCH DECENTRALIZATION CAN THE PARTY AFFORD?

Decentralization has now become a magic word in Eastern Europe and it is the motto of every attempt at economic reform. This is hardly surprising. A demand for decentralization is a natural reaction to the obvious inadequacies of the existing overcentralized setup. But there is another reason: the growing realization that the old economic system has outlived its usefulness. Even some top party leaders in Eastern Europe have publicly said as much. Czechoslovakia's economic boss Drahomir Kolder, for instance, admitted quite frankly:

> We realize now that the main source of the negative trends which have accompanied the development of our economy in the last few years is the conflict between new requirements for the economic growth of our economy and the obsolete system of planning and management, which is not in line with contemporary and long-term future needs of our economy. (76)

The same trend of thinking is clearly discernible in other Moscow bloc countries. In Poland the demand for greater economic autonomy of individual enterprises was written into the reform program adopted at the Polish Party Congress in June 1964 (191). In Hungary *Nepszabadsag* summed up a two-month debate on the blueprint of economic reform: "There was full agreement among the debaters that what is needed is not a patching up but an all-out reform. The guiding concept of this reform is: the effective coupling of commodity-money relations, i.e., an increase in the role of the market, combined with economic planning and, in connection with these, an increase in the independence of the individual enterprise" (122).

The real issue today is not whether decentralization is necessary or not, but a far more subtle one: how much decentralization the party can afford. The dilemma facing party authorities in Eastern Europe is how to make a reformist omelet without breaking too many eggs. There is mounting pressure from various quarters for scrapping all the apparatus of centralized management, while the party establishment, although acknowledging the obvious need for some degree of decentralization, fears it may go too far. This is because it is extremely difficult to distinguish between the political and the economic effects of the proposed reform measures.

From the viewpoint of Marxist economic theory, as well as from political power considerations, the old centralized structure of the economy was more consistent with the communist conception of a one-party oligarchy. By concentrating in its hands total political power, as well as all the essential economic prerogatives, the party elite was able to prevent the growth of rival power groups while at the same time enjoying a free hand in the economic sphere. Incidentally, of course, this system gave the "new class" all the material perquisites that go with a monopoly of power.[1] From the point of view of the party elite, the traditional system of economic centralism had every advantage except one: it did not work very well once the economy got beyond the stage of absolute scarcities.

Radoslav Selucky, a well-known Czechoslovak economist, described rather well the reasons why the bulk of the bureaucratic apparatus identified itself with the traditional centralized structure of the economy:

> The administrative system suited its mentality almost to an ideal degree. It defined jobs and technological processes, it created comfortable and easily repeated stereotypes. Just think how this system managed to find work for thousands of people: the assignment alone of the tasks in the plan, the weekly, monthly, quarterly and annual returns absorbed millions of hours of work which, from the aspect of an efficient operation of the economy, were entirely unproductive. All

---

[1] This issue is discussed at length in the well-known book *The New Class* by Milovan Djilas.

this meant the completion of forms, the manipulation of indices, an enormous flow of information which was essentially useless, since it did not convey anything that is required for the efficient management of production. Was there any sense in this work? Objectively seen, there was not. However, the individual must be able to feel that his work has a purpose. Therefore, he pretends that he carries out important duties without which society cannot exist, although, in actual fact, he could have replaced this cumbersome regulated work of people through automatic regulation. (42)

Much to the regret of all those bureaucrats, this old system is gradually being abandoned and one can well understand the reservations and apprehensions with which the party establishment faces the devolution of responsibilities. For a great majority of its members, the problem is one not only of ideological conviction and political power, but often of bread and butter.[2] And therefore the issue involved is of a fundamental nature. Is the present party establishment capable of carrying out a pragmatic economic reform involving a decentralization not only of economic decision-making but of real political power? If not, what is to be sacrificed—a substantial part of the establishment, or any meaningful change in the economic system? So far only the Yugoslavs have faced up to this dilemma. As Edvard Kardelj put it:

In practice we encounter resistance in some Party organizations and this resistance is more or less along the line of preserving statist-centralist forms of appropriation, so that all funds can be distributed through political channels. (251)

A Central Committee resolution in March 1966 warned party members to stop opposing the reform program:

The leaders and organizations of the League of Communists must take measures against those members and communists who are protagonists of bureaucratic and nationalistic tendencies, as well as against those who, in an opportunist manner, side with misdirected tendencies and petty-bourgeois disorientation, thus degrading true humanitarianism and liberty. . . . The reform renders the problem of responsibility more acute in a quite concrete manner. The League of Communists should energetically clear away all deviations from the program and attitudes of the Eighth Party Congress. (250)

---

[2] This problem is discussed in more detail in Chapter 6.

Yugoslavia is so far the only country which appears willing to carry decentralization through to its logical conclusion. Of course the necessity is argued (on purely economic grounds) in other countries. But neither the party leaders nor a substantial portion of the "new class" are yet ready to surrender their basic prerogatives of economic control for the sake of economic efficiency (32). Instead, some of the directive functions of the central planners are being handed down to a lower level of the bureaucracy, i.e., to trusts or industrial associations. This represents a certain degree of progress, and in the long run the new organizational superstructure may indeed prove to be less bureaucratic and more responsive to the demands of the market. But it is not a victory for decentralization.

This very point has been made quite forcibly by Eugen Loebl, one of the more extreme protagonists of economic reforms in Czechoslovakia.[3] In a long study published in the Slovak literary weekly *Kulturny Zivot*, he warns that the new economic model may flounder because of the continuing gross interference of central institutions into the affairs of individual enterprises. Asserting that "macro-economy still rules micro-economy," he cites many examples to show how centralist interference breeds even more control and argues that the situation can be remedied only if the individual enterprises are granted the largest possible degree of independence.

Loebl is particularly concerned over the very limited degree of enterprise independence. This, in his opinion, is due to the circumstance that the central authorities, ministries, and branch managements are indiscriminately applying macro-economic considerations to the micro-economy, though the latter is a very different sphere. Such a policy, Loebl argues, is not only in itself harmful but also produces a chain of additional interference on the part of the center, thus strengthening its position to the detriment of enterprise independence and paralyzing the sound forces of the reform.

As for superior agencies, Loebl is dissatisfied with the way in

[3] Eugen Loebl, given a life sentence at the Slansky trial in 1952, released four years later, and formally rehabilitated in 1963, is now manager of the Bratislava branch of the State Bank. Ever since the 1963 liberalization he has ranked among the foremost and most courageous of the reformers.

which they have come into being. He does not deny the need for the existence of higher economic organs, but argues that branch managements should have been created by the enterprises themselves, not administratively established by the center. It is precisely because the rights of branch managements were delegated to them by the center that the independence of enterprises "has become illusory." The proper procedure would have been for largely independent enterprises to cede the functions which they cannot cope with to branch managements or the center—in other words, a process diametrically opposed to that actually introduced. The continuing attempts to solve everything from the macro-economic standpoint harbor the danger of a return to the old regimentation.

There is, no doubt, much justification for this type of criticism, but this does not alter the fact that some progress has been made. To get a clear picture of what is happening one must compare the new organizational structure with the traditional one. The old chain of command was run along military lines, with all powers of economic decision making reserved for the party leadership. In practice, of course, this exalted body dealt only with basic overall economic decisions and left the central planners to translate those decisions into specific and detailed instructions for the lower echelons of the economic bureaucracy. But those directives were still subject to control and scrutiny from the top, even to the actual number of houses to be built or the assortment of shoes to be produced. The lower organs of economic bureaucracy were only transmission belts; they had no more right to depart from their directives than a battalion or company commander has to ignore the orders of his superiors.

The military simile is more than appropriate here since the communists tend to regard every economic activity as a kind of struggle—a "battle for bread" or a "battle for steel." But unlike good generals, the communist planners were concerned not only with strategic concepts and final objectives but with the actual deployment of companies and platoons. The plan directives that went out to the individual ministries were like thick catalogues, crammed with every kind of detail. The logistics of raw material supply, the most minute specifications for goods to be produced, dozens of indices covering everything from wages to productivity

—all of these were centrally determined. The basic function of the ministry was to prepare still more detailed instructions for various branches of the industry it controlled, and hand them down to the appropriate central board which in turn allocated the concrete production tasks to individual enterprises.

The emerging organizational pattern has a different shape. As a rule (for there are significant differences among the various schemes), the central planners are to be shorn of many of their former prerogatives. In terms of our military simile, most tactical decisions are now to be made at a lower level while the top echelon is to concentrate on broad strategic concepts and on so-called "perspective planning." But a new institutional superstructure has been created: the so-called industrial associations or manufacturing economic organizations.[4]

These new institutions are perhaps best described as a cross between an old-fashioned cartel, a combine (often both vertical and horizontal), and a holding company. Like any holding company, the new "trust" has full control of the finances of its component enterprises. But its primary tasks are organizational. Like an old-fashioned cartel, or a modern industrial combine, it is to distribute production tasks and pass upon the production plans of its dependent enterprises. In fact, the new "trusts" are meant to take over most (but not all) of the controlling powers formerly exercised by the central planners (139). One might say—returning to military terms—that the old unwieldy army corps has been replaced by smaller, more mobile brigades; but this change in the upper command structure does not necessarily give more independence to individual company commanders.

The new bureaucratic units are certainly smaller and organized on more rational lines. But whether they will also function in a more rational way is not yet clear. The most one can say is that the new chain of economic command should be given the benefit of the doubt.

Some of the East European reformers have also serious misgivings on this very issue. At a conference of Polish economists held in Wisla in April 1966, the proper role of the middle-level

---

[4] There is one exception to this rule. Such a middle-level superstructure will apparently be dispensed with in Hungary.

superstructure was apparently the most hotly debated problem. According to an official report:

> The above question caused the biggest worry at the conference. Today it is no longer enough to state that the scope of prerogatives (of an industrial association) should depend on the concrete conditions in a given branch of industry, depending on the kind of production involved and its connections with the customers. The question was asked whether the increase of the prerogatives of industrial associations will be accomplished at the cost of enterprises, or whether the ministries would also hand over some of their own prerogatives. It was pointed out at the conference that, so far, the only visible trend is to reduce the independence of enterprises. Facts were cited showing that enterprises were being deprived of the right to make decisions which can properly be made only on the level of an enterprise.
>
> This creates a number of dilemmas. The enterprise is supposed, after all, to remain the basic economic unit, a legal entity, working according to the principle of economic cost accounting. The managers of enterprises are held responsible for the economic results. On the other hand, industrial associations will have the right to establish plan targets and financial norms, to change targets in the course of a year and also to transfer funds from one enterprise to another.
>
> The opinions of the members of the conference in Wisla were fairly unanimous and this was expressed in the resolution. It was stated that "exceeding these prerogatives might weaken the economic thinking, invention and feeling of responsibility for economic achievement of the personnel of the enterprise." (147)

One thing, however, must be said in favor of the new bureaucratic superstructure. Its institutions have not been set up mechanically. The specific conditions of each branch of industry were apparently (at least to some degree) taken into account. For instance in Czechoslovakia only four manufacturing economic organizations were created out of the former Ministry of Fuel and Power, while nineteen were set up in the more diversified machine-
superstructure in Czechoslovakia is (62):
building industry. The proposed subdivision of the old industrial

Fuel and power	8
Metallurgy and mining	4
Engineering	19
Chemistry and paper	5
Consumer goods and food	40
Building and building materials	14

The precise number of trusts to be created in each branch of industry is not very important. The fact remains that the new superstructure (although still overgrown) seems to be organized on more functional lines. In such industries as ore-mining and metallurgy, and in a large part of the chemical and machine-building industries, the trusts extend vertically from raw materials to final product, while in industries where individual factories produce essentially the same kind of products they have been integrated horizontally. The latter is true especially of the fuel and power, consumer goods, and food industries. On the other hand, in small local industries such as building materials (with the exception of large cement works) purely territorial criteria have prevailed. This variety of forms is itself a step in the right direction.

But diversity of form has not been matched by diversity of function (164). The tasks and prerogatives of every trust are to be basically the same, with a strong emphasis on administrative and financial control rather than actual entrepreneurship. There is thus a built-in bureaucratic bias which is bound to hamper the economic effectiveness of the new chain of command. The fact that the director of the trust is, as a rule, appointed and recalled by the minister concerned and reports to him on all aspects of his trust's activities, tends to preserve the old "transmission belt" relationship between the former seats of economic power and the new organizational superstructure (32).

Here again the human element is bound to play a much bigger role than the actual statutory provisions. The really decisive factor, at least in the transitional stage, will be the caliber of the people whose task it will be to put the new system into effect. Here, it must be said, experience has not been very encouraging. In the overwhelming majority of cases, the top and medium-grade positions in the new industrial superstructure have been taken over by people from the old bureaucratic apparatus, from the dissolved central boards or their equivalents. "Only the name of the institution on the door has been changed," a Polish journalist wrote. "The persons inside and their habits and attitudes remain the same (139).

In 1965 the Polish weekly *Polityka* sent a reporter to survey the effects of those structural changes throughout the whole Moscow bloc. He visited five countries—Bulgaria, Hungary, Czechoslovakia, East Germany, and the Soviet Union—and found everywhere that "the implementation of the new economic model is hampered by the refusal to abandon the traditional bureaucratic style of work" (156). There was an obvious reluctance on the part of the top personnel of the trusts to adapt themselves to the new conditions; decentralization was not being matched by a corresponding increase in the degree of initiative allowed to the enterprise managers. A Hungarian economist complained of the growing practice of applying a double standard in calculating profitability, one at the enterprise level and another at the trust level.

The main conclusion of the *Polityka* survey was that the governing bodies of the new industrial superstructure are not only acquisitive but they are also largely staffed by old-guard functionaries without proper qualifications for the role they were intended to play. Their resistance has blunted the effect of the new procedures—a fact which they in turn exploit as an argument against extending the scope of the reform. There have even been attempts to reverse the trend. The reporter noted, for instance, that certain enterprise targets abolished by the central planners had been re-imposed or replaced by others at the trust level.

Another Polish periodical recently reported a classic example of a collision between market-oriented reformers at the enterprise level and die-hard bureaucrats in the trust offices (157). The story deserves to be told at some length because it shows how the low caliber of the managers, and their ingrained bureaucratic outlook, run counter to the pragmatic concepts on which the new organizational pattern has been based.

The Zabrze-Zakrzow Metal Works produces refrigerators. In 1965 the enterprise management noted that the demand for refrigerators of 100 and 120 liters capacity was rapidly declining, while that for smaller refrigerators was rising. Nevertheless they were forced by the trust to stick to their old production plan, and soon their warehouses were jammed with unsold products. The enterprise management, in a joint session with the workers' council, decided that in its 1966 production plan the output of the smaller models should be raised by 70 per cent at the expense of the larger ones.

This seemed only common sense. There is no point in producing goods customers do not want. But the proposed production plan of the Zabrze-Zakrzow Metal Works was flatly rejected by the trust. In a detailed directive sent down by the bureaucrats, the factory was ordered to increase its output of large-size refrigerators above the 1965 level. The reason given was that the manufacture of small units takes relatively more labor, and to reach the target for value of total output the enterprise would have to hire more workers or pay more overtime to its present workers. This would conflict with the indices for wages and employment already worked out by the trust and approved by the ministry. On the other hand, by producing only the larger refrigerators (for which, let us remember, there was little demand and of which some 60,000 were already in stock) the enterprise in Zabrze would be able to achieve its target for value of total output and keep within its prescribed wage and employment limits (157).

As long as this sort of Alice in Wonderland economic thinking still prevails at the level of the trusts, or industrial associations, one may ask the question: have the structural reforms carried out so far achieved anything? What is the use of a formal decentralization, which merely replaces index-oriented directives of the central planners by equally unrealistic dictates of the lower echelon of economic bureaucracy?

This is by no means a specific Polish problem. So far only three countries of the Soviet bloc have advanced to a stage at which one can discuss the practical experiences of the new system. There is little critical material from East Germany—either because the system there is more efficient, or more probably because Ulbricht allows less criticism. But in Czechoslovakia the same phenomenon of bureaucracy reasserting itself is clearly discernible. The "father" of the new economic model, Professor Ota Sik, has attributed the slow progress of the reform to the emergence of *dirigiste* habits in the new superstructure. Sik complained that although the number of directive indices imposed on the enterprises by their superior organs has been cut in compliance with the basic concepts of the NEM, the managers of individual factories are still not free to make meaningful economic decisions and to exercise the proper degree of entrepreneurship. This, says Sik, results from the fact that the trusts have replaced former "directive indices" by a new set of "orientation indices" which play much the same role (48).

Since the *dirigiste* type of bureaucratic attitude tends to perpetuate itself at every level of the industrial superstructure, the question naturally arises whether a communist type of planned economy can ever rid itself of the centralist bug. Certainly structural changes alone, however well meant, are not an answer to this intricate problem. First of all a lot of theoretical spadework on the proper role of the "socialized enterprise" as the backbone of the new economic system is necessary. Like other problems of micro-economics, this issue has been almost totally neglected by Marxist theoreticians. Only in Poland has there been any real attempt to tackle this problem seriously and to define the role of the individual enterprise in other than generalities (201).

In the traditional concept of the planned economy the individual enterprise had a purely functional, productive character. Its role was to provide the planners monthly, quarterly, or annually with a predetermined assortment of goods. Distribution of the goods (except for delivering them to the appropriate state warehouse) was not the concern of the enterprise director, nor were such basic elements of business costs as wage rates, prices of raw materials and fuel, etc. He did not work for the final consumer nor even for the wholesalers or retailers. He worked for the central planners (35). In this kind of planned economy there was no need for diversity of functions at the intermediate level. The director of a coal mine, an auto factory, or a food-packing plant all had essentially the same job: to deliver the goods according to specifications, or else.

Thus there was no need to work out a theory on the proper role of the individual enterprise. One does not need a theory on the use of a pressure cooker, one simply cooks one's meal and that is the end of it.

In the new system the tasks and prerogatives of individual enterprises are, or ought to be, diversified to a considerable degree. The degree of autonomy one can grant to a synthetic fiber plant and, say, to a furniture factory cannot be the same. Nor can the functional pattern of the superstructure (145). And here we come to the root of the trouble, as pinpointed by Poland's Professor Lipinski (164). The essence of the new model is that it requires a variety of structural, functional, and organizational patterns, including a greatly diversified chain of command. Instead there is a drive toward uniformity of functions, based on a purely schematic pattern of decentralization. If such a uniform superstructure is staffed by people of inherent bureaucratic leanings, the result is a foregone conclusion.

To a Western mind it is obvious that one has to apply various patterns of organizational structure to different branches of industry. There may be valid economic reasons for superimposing a trust structure on, say, coal mines. There is no logic in putting a soda water factory and a brick kiln under one institutional control simply because they happen to be in the same locality. But under present "decentralization" patterns this is exactly what has happened to small local enterprises.

The problem is not only organizational. Decentralization can never be really effective so long as the superstructural institutions attempt to "run" their subordinate enterprises and usurp for themselves essential economic functions which belong to the lower level. This is not only a question of habits and attitudes of bureaucrats but also of economic priorities. Under any system there are bound to be conflicts between "producers" on the factory level and those who make managerial decisions (35). This is because they have different criteria of economic efficiency. But in a market economy these differences tend to be resolved by the pragmatic tests of sales and profits.

The traditional communist-planned economy had its own priorities: the requirements of a high growth rate and of fulfilling the indices of the national plan. But the new emphasis on consumer demand (at least at the enterprise level) has produced a conflict of priorities. The enterprise director is now expected to serve two masters: his customers and the bureaucrats above him. This often places him in an impossible position in which he cannot pay proper attention to the requirements of the market without running afoul of his superiors from the trust who still regard themselves as the custodians of the plan.

The Czechoslovak economist Eugen Loebl described this type of situation in the following manner:

> The enterprise directors do not have the sense of full responsibility for the management of their enterprises. This is the consequence of the fact that, to a decisive degree, they have no right to be masters of their enterprises' fate, which makes them feel that the enterprise which they manage is actually not their enterprise; thus there is a kind of alienation between the top men in the enterprise and the enterprise

itself. They manage the enterprise in accordance with directives, orders and instructions which they did not work out themselves and about which they have little to say.

It cannot be expected that the top men in our enterprises, who are certainly realistically thinking people, do not realize that the majority of the measures introduced by the supervising bodies are dictated by macro-economic considerations and that it is these considerations which dominate the measures which affect so thoroughly the fate of every enterprise. These measures channel the activity of the top men in every enterprise in a direction in which they don't want to go at all. The principle of enterprise independence, one of the main principles of the new system, is in practice eliminated—to the detriment of economic growth. (35)

One might argue that since the declared objective of all the economic reforms is to better satisfy the needs of the market, all that is needed is a change in the outlook and habits of the people on the trust level. Once the higher echelons of the industrial superstructure acquire the necessary market-oriented business outlook—and this, after all, may be only a question of time—the new system could be expected to work reasonably well. This seems to be the thinking of the more pragmatic members of the party hierarchy. Thus Rezso Nyers, supervisor of Hungary's economic reform, wrote some time ago that the basic aim of all the new measures is to strengthen the independence of individual enterprises. Some degree of central control, wrote Nyers, is of course bound to remain but the manner of its implementation must change. Administrative control will be replaced by indirect control through economic levels: the market mechanism, price and income policy, investment credits, and tax measures (113).

But there is still the question how much bureaucratic residue will remain in this central control, and particularly to what extent the demands of the market and the other levers of "indirect control" will be allowed to influence decisions in the corridors of power.

One can argue *ad infinitum* the theoretical advantages and disadvantages of "indirect control" versus "administrative direction." But in practice the problem can be reduced to more simple terms. It is not so much a question of who makes the decisions as on what premises those decisions are based. If decentralization is to be effective it cannot be restricted to the problem of what to produce at the enterprise level. Rather, it involves fostering an attitude of real entrepreneurship and market orientation at all levels of the economic hierarchy (164).

This means that a factory director must be able not only to decide whether to produce large or small refrigerators, but also to switch from refrigerators to electric cookers or vacuum cleaners in response to market demand. He must also have the power to set (or negotiate) his own wage scales and his own selling prices (145, 56). He should also have the right to expand his factory through appropriate investments if conditions warrant. Only then could one speak of full autonomy of the individual enterprise.

This does not mean that the trust superstructure would become superfluous, or that there would be no need for central planners. Under any kind of economic system certain overall economic decisions (such as how much the country will consume out of its total income and how much it will invest) are in fact made at the central level. In addition there are always matters of national priority which must receive first considerations. The authorities could not be expected to give up these essential functions and prerogatives. The problem of economic control from the center (and at the medium superstructure level) is not one of kind but of degree.

As far as the individual enterprise's assortment of output is concerned, the authorities in Eastern Europe seem to have accepted the principle that this should be eventually determined at the factory level. In the long run this may well come to pass despite the resistance of the trust superstructure. But it still will not be enough if it means that the refrigerator factory would go on producing refrigerators (although determining their size and perhaps even their selling price). The problem of enterprise autonomy cannot be reduced to output and price determination. There is, for instance, the much more complex problem of allocating investment funds (25).

Under the traditional system all investment decisions were reserved for the central planners, who maintained an iron control over capital resources. The new model assigns these prerogatives not only to the central planners but also to the trust and the enterprise. This seems logical enough. The central planners and the trust superstructure must of necessity retain all investment decisions which involve new industrial capacity (establishing new plants and new industries). But capital expenditure connected with the expansion of existing enterprises, with retooling, replacement, etc., ought to be left to enterprise directors.

But will it? So far there is every indication that the trust superstructure intends to maintain strict control (including the veto power) over all investment prerogatives vested theoretically in the enterprise directors. The much-heralded new methods of investment financing through interest-bearing bank loans do not affect the issue, however rational they may be. If anything, the immediate effect of these new methods is to reduce the level of enterprise investment by making capital too expensive (175). The real problem is not one of methods of financing, but rather of investment prerogatives and, first of all, of investment criteria.

The reforms have failed as yet to provide objective criteria for a rational investment policy. There are several reasons for this. First, the value of the currency is still purely arbitrary so that investors cannot compare costs and prices with those of other countries. They cannot say therefore whether a given investment proposal is "profitable" or not. Secondly, the arbitrary system of prices (which conceals real production costs) renders all attempts to measure the comparative effectiveness of investment alternatives completely unreliable. In the third place there is no direct relationship between investment expenditure and the profits realized from it. Hence the purely arbitrary character of all investment decisions (25). Politically speaking, this gives the superstructure bureaucrats an obvious advantage, since the people at the enterprise level cannot counter arbitrary directives with estimates of the real effectiveness of their own investment proposals.

This investment policy impasse, due to centralist and arbitrary control of all capital investment projects, has prompted a Slovak economist to express the following critical assessment:

> The causes for the failure of capital investment in our economy may be found in the fact that: a) the criteria of economic effectiveness of investments are not economically reliable, and b) there is no adequate economic mechanism in the investment policy which would stimulate, on every level and in every stage of development, maximal efficiency of every investment project.

We have quite a good idea about the shortcomings of the directive-administrative management of the investment policy. The economic efficiency of the investments earmarked and financed from the state budget actually has no real economic meaning. Unfortunately, the criteria of the sphere of capital investment, already based on the principles of the new system, suffer from the subjective and objective compromises conserving the inadequate and insufficient method of establishing the effectiveness of investments, as well as the dual, and not very efficient, mechanism of directing the investment policy. Thus the conflict between the paramount purpose of investment as the accelerator of the structural changes of the dynamically growing economy and the low standard of the management of production of the basic funds in the present conditions of the new system of management, now in the process of introduction, has not only remained, it has been actually intensified (25).

Another crucial issue is that of the available investment funds. As long as the central planners continue to "rob the factories of all essential funds"—to use Tito's own expression at the February 1966 Central Committee Plenum[5]—investment prerogatives granted to enterprise managers remain meaningless. So far this problem has not become acute in the Moscow bloc countries. But if one looks at Yugoslavia, where the issue of funds appropriation resulted in a major political conflict within the party establishment, one is forced to the conclusion that effective decentralization of investment decision-making is a long way off. Without adequate investment funds at their disposal, how can people at the enterprise level respond to signals of the market mechanism?

---

[5] As reported in *Borba,* February 26, 1966.

6

★

NEW MANAGERS FOR OLD

When many decades ago Lenin formulated the slogan "Cadres decide everything," he was thinking of the way to organize a communist party. But his slogan can also be applied to a key problem of the present day in the countries of the Soviet bloc. The question of cadres, of the right men in the right places, may be decisive in the success of the economic reforms now under way.

Both the proponents and opponents of these reforms are concentrating on the introduction of a more rational planning technique and the ancillary structural changes in industrial organization and direction. The new economic model in Czechoslovakia and Hungary, the reforms now being introduced in East Germany and Poland, the Soviet reform proposals as well as the Bulgarian experiments—all have one aim: to make the communist-planned economy function more efficiently. This effort is important and should not be underrated. But even the best organizational scheme, replete with economic incentives, cannot bring about the desired effects unless it is equipped with the proper managerial cadres (98).

The fact is that the type of enterprise manager the communists have relied upon so far will not do for the new economic system. Just as the typical Western business executive of today is a completely different kind of man from his counterpart of, say, fifty years ago, so must the communists produce a new manager who will fit the requirements of today. The system of planned economy which crystallized in the Soviet Union after the first five-year plan, and in the East European countries after 1945, was based on centralized planning and directives from above. Under this system a good enterprise manager was, first of all, a conscientious executor of the detailed directives received from the central planning authorities. While it was, perhaps, considered desirable that the manager have some technical education, at least enough to make the necessary daily decisions, this was not absolutely necessary. Far more important was his willingness to carry out the instructions of his superiors, his unquestioning obedience to directives, and his possession of good political connections. He was, to put it briefly, a party hack. His superiors could be certain that all their decisions and directives would be carried out to the letter. A long party training and—let us be frank—limited intelligence and a low level of education, were a guarantee that the enterprise manager would never display excessive initiative of his own and would not feel frustrated at having to carry out absurd orders.

The old type of manager did not need to be a good business executive. Outside the purely technical sphere of the production process and apart from seeing that the plan was faithfully executed, he had few executive decisions to make. The questions of what to produce and in what quantities were taken care of in the directives he received from the central planners (96). He had no sales problems. Once the goods were produced they were no longer his concern. He did not have to worry about wage rates, production costs (in the accepted Western sense), the prices of finished products, accounts payable, profits, or the wishes of shareholders. Wages and prices were set by the state planners. His bills were paid by the state banks. His financial deficit, if any, was covered by a state subsidy. He was told by the authorities how many workers to employ, how much to pay them, how much raw material he could use, and to which warehouse he should deliver the finished product.

True, this typical factory manager of the centralized planning era had hundreds of other things to worry about, many of them unknown to Western entrepreneurs. Mountains of paperwork, rampant bureaucracy, inexplicable shortages of materials, pilfering by the employees, and deliveries of unsuitable semi-finished products. His life was by no means easy. But hardly any of those problems called for an executive mind. Far from being a captain of industry, he was in effect no more than a corporal.

The new system will require a completely different type of

man in its leading industrial posts. The director of an enterprise will cease to be the executor of instructions received from central planning authorities and will gradually become the initiator of the economic activity carried out in his enterprise (98). Where previously the main duty of an enterprise manager was faithful compliance with the indicators of the plan imposed from above, he will now have to decide what ought to be produced and in what quantities and also be responsible for the sale of the finished products. Previously he was just a production manager, now he is to become a business executive. Special training will be more useful than a party card; the ability to predict the needs of the market and quick reaction to the fluctuation of demand will be more important than political influence.

How many of the old managers have these qualities and can reasonably be expected to cope with the more exacting duties which the new economic system will bring? Not many. One might draw an analogy between the old-style communist enterprise and an old-fashioned family business. While in the latter leading positions were reserved, as a rule, for members of the family, in the nationalized enterprise they went to card-carrying hacks, more often than not without any regard for managerial abilities. Even the most gifted outsider could break into this closed circle only by joining the party—the communist equivalent of marrying the boss's daughter.

Since communists give politics priority over economics, the best party brains were always drafted for political and ideological work. Security and the state apparatus skimmed off the second-best human material, leaving mainly third-rates for the managerial positions in industry and trade. This was all right as long as the most suitable enterprise manager was the non-commissioned-officer type, but now times are changing. One of Czechoslovakia's top economists, Radoslav Selucky, complained bitterly about the generally low quality of enterprise managers in his country:

> The old system of centralized planning leaves behind a highly unsatisfactory state of affairs with respect to the structure of qualifications of our leading technical and industrial cadres. Statistics throw harsh light on this point. The job of enterprise director will be the key post in our New Economic Model. It is essential that those holding such responsible posts be capable . . . entrepreneurs and sales executives,

that they follow closely the trend of technological development and react quickly to constant changes in demand. All this cannot be done without adequate education, without adequate business experience, without organizational abilities and without superb qualities of leadership. (43)

Lack of adequate education is indeed the Achilles heel of the old type of enterprise manager. Precise statistics are hard to find, but it is clear that a high percentage of enterprise directors have no more than an elementary education and that a correspondingly small percentage have graduated from a university. This point was stressed by the Czechoslovak party organ *Rude Pravo* which pointed out that "the majority of executives in Czechoslovak industry do not possess the necessary qualifications" and that at the deputy-director level "only 23 per cent of the existing cadres possess the skill required." At the same time "of all Czechoslovaks with higher education between the ages of 25 and 59, only 11 per cent hold leading positions in industry at the director or deputy-director level, while more than half of the university graduates are unable to find jobs which correspond to their qualifications" (53). Similar conditions prevail in Poland where about 80 per cent of the leading managers lack proper qualifications and at the same time university graduates are hired as minor office employees (158).

This preponderance of unqualified people in the leading managerial positions is a primary reason for the low economic effectiveness of East European industry. The party hack simply cannot cope with the demands of modern technology and the complex duties of the business executive. The need for a major shake-up in management has by now been generally acknowledged in all the more developed countries of the bloc. But this poses two crucial questions: first, how to get rid of the present incumbents and second, where to find the new men to replace them (98).

The second problem is by far the more difficult. Modern business executives cannot be mass produced. Apart from natural abilities, they need sound education and long business experience. The problem was well put by the Czechoslovak economist Eugen Loebl:

It is necessary to beware of the illusion that the new type of factory director will emerge naturally from the new forms of management, just as the old type was the natural product of dogmatism in economic thinking. Unfortunately the process does not reverse itself. It is relatively easy to forbid people to think and to make it impossible for them to show their ideas and abilities, but creative thinking and business acumen cannot be commanded. Hence, we must realize that we need a new type of business leader, we must appoint to the leading positions those who are of the required type and we must devote all our attention to the establishment of the most favorable conditions for the development of capable managers and give them the opportunity to show their mettle.(34)

It is easier said than done. There is still the crucial problem of how to get rid of the party hacks, as well as where to find the material for the new type of business executive. And there is also the question of how to deal with the frustration of the managers during the long transitional period between the initiation of economic reforms and its fruition. The established party hacks are bound to be apprehensive and distrustful of everything which changes their customary routine, while the new executives are equally bound to be exasperated by the unavoidable residue of old administrative methods.[1]

This frustration was underlined very forcibly in a discussion among a group of industrial managers organized by the editorial board of *Polityka*, Poland's leading political weekly.[2] Some of the participants, especially the younger and better educated managers, made no attempt to conceal their frustration, as well as their envy of their opposite numbers in the West:

Manager I: I think it is impossible to compare the director's post in our country with that in the West. One is manager of either a capitalist or of a socialist business. It can be said, in general, that the limitation of the role of the business, and hence of the role of the director, in the socialist business enterprise is justified; his subordination to the supervising authorities is indispensable, but only within the limits outlined by social interest. Unfortunately, it would appear that, under our conditions, businesses do not have enough freedom, they are not

---

1 See S. Bocz (98): "Some of the managers opposing the reform are afraid of the prospect of greater responsibility. They also fear that it may be discovered that they are not suited for the positions they now occupy. They realize that the time of comfort-loving and inefficient men is over. . . ."

2 "The Captains of Industry," a transcript of a round-table discussion with several managers, *Polityka* (April 17, 1965).

independent enough, and this makes the task of the director extremely difficult.

Manager II: I am not a manager. A manager in the West is a businessman. If he is a bad businessman, he is fired. It is not my task to raise the income of my enterprise. I do not get my salary for this. I am paid for implementing the plan in accordance with the indices received, and I am evaluated according to the indices. The man who implements directives is good. This is how I see the main difference between the real manager and the director in our country. . . .

Manager III: I once found in a professional periodical (I am speaking about the art of management) an article in which the author described the attributes required of a director in the US. They are very close to those which our directors should have. I see a difference only in the fact that in the socialist state, the director must represent at one and the same time, the interests of the state and the interests of the personnel, of the lower echelons. This can be done, but only with great difficulty. A director who does not have the professional and moral qualifications will not be able to fulfill this task. . . . The director should not accept from the state or the Association tasks which are unrealistic or which could harm the enterprise.

Very often, although we are of a different opinion than our supervisors, we do not have the courage to say so out of fear of the consequences. . . .

Manager VII: We found a contracting party who was ready to buy carbide for $80 a ton. This export had to be paid for by an import of acetone at $100 a ton, but as four units of carbide have to be used for one unit of acetone, the profit was obvious. It was possible to earn, or to save, whichever you prefer, $220,000. But the whole thing got stuck in Warsaw. There has been no decision taken and those $220,000 are melting away at the rate of $10,000 a week (the deadlines, the production potential, etc., being decisive here). Can the director's personal attitude, his determination, courage, effort, and energy get him anywhere in such a situation? It all depends on the person you come up against in Warsaw.

Manager VIII: I know this case, and from the Warsaw end at that. The case reached the necessary deputy minister and, judging from my knowledge of him, it would have been settled immediately had this been in his power. But it wasn't. He had to take the matter to the central office in question and deal with somebody from the Ministry of Foreign Trade. That man, in turn, had to discuss the case with another person, and with still another who was away or very busy with something else.

Such experiences, which after all are the daily fare of any enterprise manager in Eastern Europe, are bound to discourage new men from coming forward. Loebl, in his article cited above (34), urged that every effort be made to find capable entrepreneurs, put them into leading positions and create conditions in which they can apply their abilities. But will such men stay in their posts while bureaucracy has the upper hand? And if they do, will they retain their drive and their acumen over the long transitional period?

The problem of frustration and the feeling of helplessness in the face of the omnipotent and anonymous bureaucratic system is not confined to enterprise managers. It is also apparently shared by some of the directors of the industrial associations. Here, for instance, is an extremely characteristic statement made by one of such dignitaries in an interview published in *Zycie Gospodarcze:*

Editor: Has the scope of responsibilities which you undertake independently, for which you are personally responsible, increased since the resolution of the Council of Ministers concerning the greater independence of industrial associations? If so, in what direction; if not, why not?

Director: To be quite frank, I must say that in my position I have noticed no difference. There are no new prerogatives, no new duties which would help in industrial management in a more effective way. The scope of decisions which I can make has remained identical, as it was before. So it is in everyday practice. This does not mean that nothing is being done about preparing new methods of management, that we are not fighting for their implementation. The problem is not easy; we tried it some years ago without any great success. Today we are hampered frequently by simple bureaucracy. Nothing new? This is true, but it is equally true that this nightmare has taken very strong hold. It is not easy to fight it. The entire apparatus (I do not mean the people, but the forms and the methods) is stiff, dogmatic and "paper-bound." Over the years, methods of operation have taken hold and we are unable to get away from them. No one has the power and—in a certain sense—the courage. I must say that the general shortcoming of the system is the lack of trust in people at the lower administrative echelons. After all, if a person has been appointed a director, he must have appeared trustworthy. And yet, frequently when I should make decisions and be responsible for them, the decisions are made "above," sometimes after consulting me and sometimes without consultation. This is often absurd. In the last two months I lost perhaps 40 per cent of my time in unnecessary conferences with people who—in many cases—know nothing about "the business." The trend to increase the independence of industrial associations is justified. It must be implemented consistently; we must be given a greater freedom of movement. (180)

But even assuming that this greater freedom of movement is granted and that the party is able to refurbish the top ranks of industry with a new type of executive, there remains the problem of how to get rid of the old type. This is primarily a political issue. In the communist system the distribution of top-level jobs is based on political patronage to an extent unheard of in other countries. The question is not so much one of "jobs for the boys" as one of finding good and well-paid positions for the protegés of this or that party dignitary. And lucrative jobs in industrial management do not go to the rank and file. Such positions are given, as a rule, to well-connected people who cannot be removed for mere incompetence without bitter internal infighting.

When and if they are removed, the question remains what to do with them. The great majority of them are over fifty but still in the active age groups. They would hardly be willing to return to the low-grade production jobs from which they were elevated (158). They have acquired a taste for power, for authority, and for good living. The party apparatus proper cannot absorb them either. But if alternative jobs are not found for them the old-style managers may well become the "pieds noirs" of the communist regime which sacks them. In a party ridden by factionalism this could be a real political danger.

One solution would be to retain them so that "with the help of their practical experience," they could become real business executives (29). This has been done on a small scale in Poland. But for obvious reasons only a minute percentage of the hacks could be considered for this retraining scheme and the results were far from satisfactory (161). As far as the others are concerned, Warsaw seems to be following a deliberately dilatory policy and waiting until the bulk of the party hacks reach retirement age. This, after all, is the simplest way out and only the economy suffers.

The policy of delay may be more than mere opportunism. After all, these old managers performed one useful function from the standpoint of the party leadership. They were a crucial link in the party's political control over the economy, a control which every true Marxist-Leninist considers essential if the party is to stay in power. Thus one may assume that while the Novotnys, Gomulkas, and Ulbrichts accept the harsh fact that the old-time party hacks have to be gradually removed from the leading managerial posts in industry, they do not want to replace them with just anybody on the basis of pure ability. They would prefer to look for managerial timber among the young party members and train them for executive jobs in industry (61).

This kind of thinking is discernible in a document of the Central Committee of the East German Party, outlining a scheme for training young party functionaries who will be both politically reliable and specialists in technology and economics (91). The text of this resolution shows that its main purpose is to replace large numbers of old and technically unqualified apparatchiks with young, educated experts.

> The main content of the cadre program consists of . . . measures to replace those cadres who, in the long run, can no longer be equal to their future tasks for reasons of health and age, and of insufficient qualification. . . .

The document envisages a new type of functionary who would combine both academic and political qualifications; it stresses the former, however, underlining the great responsibility of the younger generation to acquire more factual and specialized knowledge.

In Hungary the campaign against party hacks began early in the 1960's when the Kadar regime started appointing non-party experts to important administrative posts. Kadar provided the political rationale with his famous slogan in 1962, "Whoever is not against us is with us." This policy brought widespread opposition at the lower levels of the party, particularly from those whose positions were endangered. Their attitude—"it was we who worked and fought for the party, not these others"—was criticized by the party newspaper *Nepszabadsag* on March 16, 1962:

> It is mostly from the untalented, inefficient people that we see the greatest opposition. They are fully aware how unfavorably they compare with the more talented and better trained, and this is the

reason for their attacks. Knowing well that this attitude is contrary to party policy, they dress their complaints in political garb. (112)

The opposition of party hacks continued during 1963, and *Nepszabadsag* was led to comment again on June 29:

Until after the 1956 counter-revolution and during the fight for the dictatorship of the proletariat, political purity was of primary importance. However, it is a mistake to continue, on the basis of political integrity, to camouflage illiteracy; because those who cannot keep in step with vocational progress hinder constructive progress even if they are paragons of political reliability at their posts. Not that we don't need political firmness; we certainly do, but that is not enough. The complicated task of constructing socialism needs both firmness and expert knowledge. (101)

This aim has not been pursued so explicitly in the other countries. The Czechoslovaks, for instance, seem to make a distinction between technical jobs, which can safely be left to non-political specialists, and the truly managerial positions which—in their opinion—require political training. The following excerpt from R. Selucky's article in *Svobodne Slovo* makes this distinction clear:

The art of management requires a special talent, for the full exercise of which the manager must possess the necessary psychological and organizational qualifications, in addition to his other talents. Management is about to become a specific profession which, though based on technical (economic, legal, engineering, etc.) skill, also requires, as an essential part, an additional sum of special knowledge (in psychology and social work, in what is called human relationship, etc.). Only when the specialist possesses this special knowledge can he become a good manager. . . . Not all jobs in the management of the national economy are alike. In some, economic or technical management is connected with political activities (posts in which the material interests of individuals are decided), while other jobs are of a purely technocratic nature (the decisions made only concern the technical or technological aspect). Those who decide how the profit of the enterprise is to be distributed, combine technical and political activities in their job, while those making the decisions about the way electric current is to be fed to the grid or how steam is to be used in the big industrial combine, only engage in technical activities. It is clear that, while it is necessary to put the accent on the political aspect of the qualification in the first case, technical considerations prevail in the second. . . . (41)

But whatever its politically inspired limitations, the obvious necessity to replace party hacks with trained business executives has had one very beneficial by-product: it has made the party leaders realize the need for establishing proper management-training schemes. The communists have always prized economic achievement but have tended to hold managerial skills in contempt. This attitude has now changed, and the need for proper business and management training is gradually being accepted. In this field the Poles have pioneered the way (as they also did in that of economic reform). The National Management Training Center (Centralny Osrodek Doskonalenia Kadr Kierowniczych) was established in Warsaw in 1958 for the express purpose of directing the various managerial training schemes and promoting advanced management techniques. Between then and the end of March 1964, some 1,400 people had taken its experimental courses and more than 2,700 have participated in its seminars (196). But this apparently was only the beginning. The resolution of the July 1965 Central Committee Plenum (at which the reform program for 1966–1970 was approved) explicitly demanded that all persons occupying leading posts in economic administration should either have proper educational standards or undergo an intensive management training course (195). Even before that, specific provisions concerning the proper qualifications of some of the top managerial personnel were spelled out in the Decree of the Council of Ministers of July 29, 1964 (192). According to this decree, the competent ministries, together with the State Committee for Labor and Wages and the relevant organs of the trade unions, must define the posts which should be occupied only by economists with higher economic education. Also persons with long experience in managerial work (of at least ten years duration) would be permitted to retain their positions, if they could prove that their knowledge of economic problems permits them to carry out their functions.

The same decree obliges the ministries to improve the qualifications of the leading cadres and raise their educational standards by means of special crash training courses organized in cooperation with competent universities and professional institutes. Paragraph

7 of the decree sets a limit of five years (i.e., until 1969) as the time during which the leading personnel in the economic administration should acquire proper educational standards as required in the posts they occupy. The qualifications involved should be certified by normal examination procedure.

Elsewhere in the bloc the same trend can be noted. In December 1964 the Czechoslovak Central Committee Presidium made it clear that non-party specialists should be given preference over unqualified party card holders in filling top managerial positions:

> The Central Committee does not agree with the incorrect practice which has been adopted in some instances and which consists of preference being given to cadres with inferior qualifications and less ability, when appointments to the leading posts and positions in the administration of state and economy, or in the management of production, are made for the sole reason that these people are members of the Party. (72)

In spite of this categorical directive, "the incorrect procedure in the appointment of executives persisted by its own momentum" (63), and the Czechoslovak party authorities had to issue another warning that "those who favor a cadre practice of this kind seem to forget that . . . managerial posts in enterprises are no longer key positions in the class struggle" and that "this is a very harmful practice which causes many of the old shortcomings to persist in our national economy." At the same time the article in question tried to define the criteria of managerial ability by stating that apart from proper professional qualifications, the would-be executives "must not be afraid of making decisions and bearing responsibility for those decisions" as well as being able to spur other people "to use their initiative and abilities. A firm knowledge of psychology and sociology of labor also belong to the qualifications required of an executive." Finally, the article makes the essential point that "it is unimportant whether the candidate for an executive post is a communist or not, but it is important that he should possess all the qualifications necessary for a successful discharge of his duties."

This is the line which (as pointed out above) the Hungarian regime has been plugging in for several years. But elsewhere in the bloc the scientific training of managerial cadres is still in its infancy. The Soviet Union has organized the first State Business Administration Faculty (Fakultet Gosudarstvennogo Deloproizvodstva) at the Moscow University only in 1965.[3] Hungary plans to train some 1000–1500 executives by the end of 1967 and about 10,000 by 1970.[4] Even Rumania proposes to set up a Managerial Council, which would undertake the task of organizing proper management training (205) and has reluctantly admitted that there is such a thing as science of management (207). Thus one may assume that the supply of qualified and trained executives will increase considerably in all countries of the Moscow bloc in the not so distant future.

Presumably some of the new business executives will also have party cards in their pockets, but party membership will no longer be the main criterion for top positions in industry, although it may still be a necessary pre-condition for getting the jobs. But from the viewpoint of the old party hacks, it is immaterial who the people are who take their jobs (as well as their power and authority) away from them. The essential point is that they are going to be removed. They are fully aware of the fact that their entrenched position has been undermined by the wave of economic reform, and their natural tendency is to oppose the changes, or at least to delay them as long as possible. This is why the old managers form the backbone of the opposition to economic pragmatism. Professor Liberman, the leading Soviet exponent of economic reform, has been quoted as saying that his ideas "are being opposed with fixed bayonets by some people interested in their jobs" (228).

This opposition is only natural from people who have everything to lose. It is an important obstacle to the progress of economic reform throughout Eastern Europe. If the old managers had any qualifications it was their possession of political influence. They are now using all their pull in the fight against reform and against their own doom.

---

[3] Interview with the Dean of this new faculty, L. N. Kachalin—Radio Moscow, February 25, 1965 (see 227).

[4] The speech of K. Polinszky, Deputy Minister of Culture and Education, as reported in *Nepszabadsag* (October 17, 1966).

7

★

THE COST OF ECONOMIC REFORMS

Economic reforms have been openly discussed throughout Eastern Europe for more than a decade. But during all this time one aspect of the changeover from direct to indirect controls has been carefully avoided: the economic and social costs of such reforms. All other elements are being debated and analyzed in great detail: the role of profits, the thorny problems of investment financing, the respective merits of alternative organizational structures, the best methods of price determination, and dozens of other, often quite controversial, problems. Each of these subjects has already acquired a substantial analytical literature of its own in many East European languages. Only the problem of the price which has to be paid for putting the economic house in order still remains a taboo.

In a way this conspiracy of silence is easy to understand. The main reason why a new economic system has to be adopted throughout Eastern Europe is the pressing need to rectify the adverse effects of a chronic mismanagement of economic resources, indulged in for decades under the name of a "scientifically planned economy." Thus, the present reforms are an effort to repair the damage wrought by many, many years of a dogmatic, quasi-wartime economy and the idolatry of the golden calf of high growth rate at any price.

The communist rulers of Eastern Europe have, obviously, a very good political reason for avoiding the touchy subject of the heavy social and economic costs of the change in the economic model. Despite the frantic search for suitable scapegoats and a more or less frank confession of past sins and errors, the blame for the hardships looming ahead must be borne collectively by the whole party establishment, since in the late forties and early fifties it was the main instrument responsible for forcing an alien and dogmatic economic system on the unwilling nations of Eastern Europe. But a Western analyst is free from such guilt inhibitions. So let us pose the question: what hardships are involved in the switch-over to the new ways and methods of planning and management?

Every economic system has its own rules of the game and its own hierarchy of priorities. Economic efficiency can never be measured in absolute terms. The performance of any economy can be judged only in relation to the final objectives. Wartime economy is here a classic example. As soon as war is declared, the accepted norms of economic behavior are thrown overboard and all economic effort is subordinated to the basic objective of producing the required number of guns, tanks, and other military equipment necessary to win the war, cost what it may.

The idolatry of statistical growth rate has also its own rules and its own accepted standards. The basic norm is the absolute priority of the politically (and subjectively) determined growth rate indicators over any but the very basic needs (measured at the subsistence level) of mass consumption. Such an order of priorities permits squeezing out of the economy the maximum amount of necessary means for capital accumulation purposes. With this objective in mind, the peasants are forced to hand over their crops at a fraction of their true economic price. Workers and other employees are paid subsistence wages. Consumer goods are scarce, shoddy and (with the exception of basic food items) outrageously expensive. In addition the government resorts from time to time to the floating of forced loans and confiscation of savings.

Such drastic methods of draining the citizens' purchasing power are possible only in an authoritarian political system based on secret police terror and minute control of economic life by party bureaucracy. But mass terror and administrative control are themselves very costly weapons. They tie up a substantial portion of manpower and resources. Besides, both the terror and the control apparatuses demand their share of the spoils. Finally, the productivity of underpaid labor is notoriously very low. So, even from the purely economic point of view (quite apart from political, moral, and ethical considerations) the system of terror and direct control is bound soon to reach the point of diminishing returns.

But in the meantime the inherent evils of an arbitrary centralist and bureaucratic economic system have set in. The disregard of costs leads to over-employment of labor and squandering of capital resources. Labor productivity and investment efficiency stagnate, waste is rampant, and repressed inflation presents an ever-growing danger. All this explains why, despite their statistically imposing growth rates, the countries of Eastern Europe failed in the last twenty years to keep pace with the substantial increase in the living standards recorded throughout the Western world. The bulk of economic gains was dissipated by maintaining the apparatus of terror and control, by the high margin of waste, and by paying the enormous cost of economic inefficiency. Thus there are no reserves which could be used to offset the cost of a switch-over to a more rational system of running the national economy.

Even in an open society the changeover from an arbitrary system, based on non-economic priorities (as during wartime) is bound to be costly. People who remember the postwar years know that when a country returns to peace it faces gigantic problems of readjustment. The arms factories which seemed so important yesterday have to be set to making new things. Stocks of war materiel suddenly depreciate in value. Workers must find new jobs. And the unspent money in millions of bank accounts threatens inflation.

Similar problems now face the economic planners of Eastern Europe who have been given the task of dismantling the old command economy inherited from Stalin's day. The communist reformers, however, are likely to have a more difficult time of it. They have inherited a system that has been run for years without the regard for standards of efficiency and rationality that even a war economy should observe. Their factories are swarming with excess manpower, their price system is artificial, their wages arbitrary, their agriculture neglected and undercapitalized, and a number of big projects that looked good to the politicians have turned out to be white elephants. Over all this hangs the menace of inflation, which in Eastern Europe assumes formidable dimensions because it has been so long repressed. The transition to a new system will be difficult precisely because it involves scrapping the old central controls which, backed up by the police, kept the economy from flying apart. The consumer and the manager are now to have a bigger say in running the economy, but this is easier said than done.

One of the first hazards the reformers must face is that of mass unemployment, a problem that the planners never had to worry about in the past. It is a well-known fact that the number of workers employed by the average socialized factory is considerably higher than a rational utilization of manpower would warrant.[1] The older system of central planning gave the factory manager no incentive to reduce his labor force. Firing the superfluous workers would not benefit the enterprise in any way, since the money saved could not be used for other purposes. Instead, he preferred to use the wage fund available to him in order to keep the workers on since they might come in handy in an emergency. Even though these superfluous workers automatically reduced the labor productivity index (output per man), they sometimes helped to fulfill the plan—and that was all that mattered.

The central planners were fully aware of this practice, but did nothing to discourage it. From their point of view, over-employment was preferable to the unemployment which would result if manpower were to be used more rationally. Unemployment, by Marxist definition, is a characteristic of the capitalist system and thus cannot exist in a scientifically planned communist economy. Better to let the enterprise employ twice as many people as necessary and pay them about half an economic wage rather than acknowledge what the ideologists said could not be.

The new economic system will bring a radical change in the use of manpower. For one thing, the long-neglected factor of cost is now to be of primary concern to every enterprise director. Labor

---

[1] The actual size of this over-employment is sometimes staggering. The management of Ursus Mechanical Works near Warsaw had invited a firm of Western efficiency experts to advise on problems of organization. The report submitted by this firm stated among other things that with better organization of work and with the application of modern time and motion study techniques, the production tasks assigned to this enterprise in the next few years could be accomplished with a labor force of only 12,400 workers instead of 22,500, which this enterprise now employs (see 173).

productivity and the profit margin are about to replace the old criterion, value of global output, in determining management decisions. Moreover, in all of the East European economic reforms an essential element is increased flexibility in employment and wages (51). For these reasons every director of a socialized enterprise will feel impelled to take a long, hard look at the size of his labor force.

Let us put ourselves in the shoes of the average factory director. Under the new system his primary task will be to ensure the profitability of his enterprise. He can do this in two ways: by reducing costs, and by raising his sales revenue. The easy answer would be to raise prices. But, at least in the initial stages of economic reform, the central planners intend to maintain rigid control over most selling prices.[2] This leaves little room for maneuver on the revenue side.

On the cost side, the alternatives will be limited. Prices of raw materials, energy, and factory equipment are also to be centrally determined. There are no major savings to be effected here. There remains only the cost of labor. Here substantial savings can be made, and the simplest way is to get rid of superfluous workers. Most factory directors are bound to choose this solution since it will enable them to maintain their output and even to increase it, while at the same time paying higher wages to the workers they retain. The increased performance of these workers should more than compensate for the lost manpower. And so the general tendency will be to employ a smaller number of better-paid workers.

These are by no means purely theoretical considerations. A tendency toward mass dismissals became quite evident in Yugoslavia in the latter part of 1965 when the decision was made to give factory managers greater leeway in determining employment and wages. Yugoslav economists estimated that the new measures introduced in July 1965 would result in the eventual discharge of over a quarter million workers (233). The same experience (though on a smaller scale) was reported from the Soviet Union: when several experimental enterprises in the motor transport industry in Moscow and Leningrad were given power to fix their

---

[2] See Chapter 4.

own wage rates and regulate employment, the immediate effect was a severe cutback in the labor force and an increase in earnings for those who remained. Discussing the results of this experiment in *Ekonomicheska Gazieta,* Minister of Finance Garbuzow gave his unqualified blessing to the policy of wholesale dismissals: "With a smaller number of employees and higher wages, the level of profit has increased considerably and part of it has been used to give incentives to the staff and to expand the enterprises" (212, p. 4). Garbuzow also noted that by getting rid of surplus manpower (and hiking the wages of the remaining workers) the experimental enterprises had raised their labor productivity 31 per cent. This is indeed an impressive result, since the dismissals had involved only about 7 per cent of the labor force. Should similar layoffs of surplus employees occur throughout the Soviet economy, there would obviously be a serious increase in unemployment.

This prospect is evidently causing some anxiety among the top Soviet leadership. At the 23rd Party Congress in March 1966, Moscow Oblast secretary Vasiliy Konotop expressed his concern about the difficulties of finding employment for workers laid off in the course of the manpower rationalization process. He said that while this was a small problem at the moment, it could become a serious one in the future. Konotop recommended "that the whole question be studied in order to work out a solution on a national scale."[3]

We can expect therefore, throughout Eastern Europe, a definite trend toward reducing the labor force in factories and also (to a lesser degree) in commercial and transport enterprises. The probable short-term effects of the economic reforms will in this respect be the same as those of any development aiming at a more rational use of manpower (such as automation). While there will be an increase in the average earnings of the remaining workers, this will hardly improve the plight of the jobless. The principal issue, therefore, is what to do with the surplus manpower once the dismissals begin on a large scale.

Surprisingly enough, Bulgaria has been so far the only East European country to acknowledge this problem in an official manner. In January 1967, the Bulgarian Council of Ministers issued

---

[3] "The Speech by V. I. Konotop," *Pravda* (April 4, 1966).

a decree which is at least a partial attempt to face the issue of large scale unemployment resulting from the implementation of economic reforms and to propose some remedies (14).

The decree underlines the duty of the management of enterprises, economic organizations, administrative departments, etc. to dismiss the workers who have become superfluous because of the introduction of new technology or better organizations, pointing to the fact that a continued employment of such workers would mean an obstacle to the growth of the productivity of labor. At the same time, the decree makes some provisions aimed at a careful and judicious selection of the workers to be dismissed.

Some directives are also given on how to ease the plight of the victims of such mass layoffs. Enterprise managers are told that they should "as far as possible help the dismissed workers to find a new place of employment." When this is impossible, the local representative of the Committee for Labor and Wages should attempt to find new jobs for the dismissed workers. Retraining courses are to be organized for those who will need new qualifications. During such courses, the laid-off workers shall be paid the same wage rates they received during their last month of employment. Such payments are to be maintained for three months, or, in exceptional cases, for up to six months.

Unemployed workers who are considered unsuitable for retraining, shall be paid their basic wage for one month and thereafter 50 per cent of this basic wage for a further five months. Thus a sort of embryo unemployment benefit has been introduced in Bulgaria. Special incentive payments are also to be offered to the dismissed workers who volunteer to enter those industries (such as mining and construction) where manpower is still scarce.

The Bulgarian decree is far from being an adequate answer to the problem of efficiency dismissals, but at least it is an attempt to face the whole issue. A far better solution, of course, would be to provide alternative employment by developing those branches of industry which have been wilfully neglected in the past. This may sound attractive on paper, but in practice it is bound to encounter serious difficulties. First of all, the East European communists are still bound to their Marxist dogmas, which make it difficult to justify a rapid expansion of consumer goods industries (the so-called Group B) at the expense of producers' goods industries

(Group A). But there is another serious obstacle to such a restructuring of the economy: any large-scale investment undertaken at an early stage of economic reform is bound to increase inflationary pressures by adding to the already existing amounts of unspendable purchasing power.

Some of the redundant workers could perhaps be placed in existing vacancies. But the bulk of such employment vacancies is either in highly skilled occupations or in unattractive and poorly paid positions. They offer only a marginal solution for the problem of laid-off workers (5).

A third possibility would involve a bloc-wide solution. This would be a mass migration of redundant manpower from labor-surplus countries (Poland, Bulgaria, and the Soviet Union) to labor-deficient ones (East Germany first of all and then Czechoslovakia). A small token labor migration from Poland to East Germany has taken place in the border regions (181), but it is not likely to achieve mass proportions. Some time ago the leading Czechoslovak party newspaper attempted to give this solution ideological respectability by publishing an article which discussed the question of labor migration within the framework of Comecon cooperation (28). The article cited figures on mass labor migration in Western Europe, particularly in the Common Market, implying that this was an example for the Comecon states. However, there seem to be serious political and ideological obstacles to this type of solution in the case of Eastern Europe.

Finally, there remains the solution chosen by Yugoslavia of permitting large-scale labor migration to the West. At the end of 1965, less than six months after the new stage of economic reform became operative, some 250,000 Yugoslav workers were already employed abroad (235), and Belgrade authorities estimate that by the end of 1967 this figure may rise to 400,000 (245).[4] At first the migration was semi-clandestine, but when the effects of the July 1965 reform began to be fully felt in the labor market the government in Belgrade gave its official blessing to the outflow. The

[4] This seems to be a realistic estimate. Apart from some 250–300,000 Yugoslav workers employed abroad, there were at the end of December 1966 another 278,000 unemployed (or 7.7 per cent of the labor force inside Yugoslavia). Cf. B. Kovacevic (233).

Yugoslav line is that any worker who wants to migrate can do so, but that the mass exodus needs to be carried out "in a more organized way" (253). This means that Belgrade wants to regulate the outflow of surplus manpower in agreement with the Western governments concerned. Such agreements have already been concluded with Sweden, France, and Austria and others are in the making.

Ideological and political objections apart, labor migration to the "capitalist" West has two big advantages. It provides an opportunity for the migrant workers to acquire higher skills, and (more important in the government's viewpoint) it brings an inflow of hard currency from foreign remittances which the people employed abroad send back to their families. Yugoslav income from this source in 1965 and 1966 was estimated at 100 million dollars (237, p. 5). From this angle the unemployment resulting from economic reforms ceases to be a liability and (through the export of manpower) becomes an asset. It is very unlikely, however, that any other country of Eastern Europe will follow the Yugoslav example and permit a migration of surplus labor to the West on any significant scale.

A substantial increase in unemployment therefore seems inevitable, at least in the early stages of economic reform. The social and economic costs will, of course, vary from country to country. Labor-surplus countries (Poland, Yugoslavia, the Soviet Union, and Bulgaria) are likely to be harder hit than the others, while East Germany on the other hand can only benefit from a more rational distribution of its scarce manpower. Short of permitting mass labor migration (preferably to the West), or, alternatively, securing a substantial influx of capital from abroad (either as investment credits or venture capital) (232), there is no way of avoiding at least a short-term spell of mass unemployment.

Negative effects can also be expected from the introduction of the new pricing system. A gradual transition to a market-oriented economy implies the eventual adoption of freely fluctuating prices, regulated by the interplay of supply and demand. For many reasons the communist regimes of Eastern Europe are not yet ready to accept such a pricing system without serious reservations and administrative safeguards. But the trend to equate the selling or the supply price with the economic value of the given commodity has already set in. This is another inevitable development. Rational use of economic resources is simply not possible "without a basic readjustment of the existing price structure" (99) (initially, perhaps, by the old-fashioned method of price fixing, but later increasingly through market mechanism). Within the framework of this readjustment, some prices may well eventually go down, especially those of semi-luxury durable consumer goods, where the prevailing exorbitant prices were established to keep down the demand and drain some of the excess purchasing power. But the general movement of the price level will be upward.

There are many reasons for this. First, in the early stages of economic reform, production costs are likely to increase sharply. This would result from the revision of supply prices—the prices charged for raw materials, energy, semi-finished products and capital equipment. Formerly these goods were supplied to all socialized enterprises at well below cost and the difference was paid by the state. One of the principles of the reforms is that this system of subsidies is wasteful and inefficient: the economy must charge realistically for raw materials, semi-finished products, fuel, the use of capital (both fixed and circulating) and eventually, perhaps, for labor (165). This is why all the reform blueprints include a revision of supply prices (but not wages) as the first step toward economic rationality. The resulting increase in production costs is bound to be reflected in higher prices further down the line.[5]

There are other forces which will also tend to push prices upward. Chief among them is the persisting imbalance between supply and demand. As long as many goods (especially the more attractive ones) are in short supply, any relaxation of price controls will be immediately felt by the consumer. Even where prices remain centrally determined, there will be a strong temptation to hike them upward either under pressure of the producers (who are, after all, supposed to show a profit), or in order to mop up excess purchasing power. The pressure exerted by enterprise directors requires no explanation. But the motives of the central planners (or their party overlords) are more complex. From their point of view the problem of prices in the early stages of economic reform is shot with basic contradictions. On one hand

[5] See Chapter 4.

there is the need to contain inflation, the legacy of the old centralist system which implies (or so it seems) a policy of keeping prices and wages down until rising production relieves the pent-up pressure (37).

But at the same time the planners are faced with rapidly growing claims on the state budget. Rationalization of the existing productive capacity requires vast new investment outlays, while the funds available to the state tend to decrease with the growing autonomy of the socialized enterprises and trusts (51). This leads the planners to seek economies in the area of so-called "nonproductive" expenditures. In this category are the various attempts at reducing public consumption (either subsidized or free) in favor of private (and fully paid-for) consumption. Various services which were formerly supplied at less than their economic cost will now carry higher price tags. Here the classic example is housing. In many countries of Eastern Europe we are now witnessing a basic reversal of the established policies in this field. For two decades the main cost of housing construction was borne by the state, the available apartments being let to carefully chosen tenants at only a nominal rent. Now some countries (Poland, for instance) have increased this rent substantially (179), and several of them require all but the poorest citizens to join housing cooperatives or to build (or buy) their own houses. This means that people must use part of their savings for down payments and in general spend a larger share of their personal income on housing.[6]

Thus in Eastern Europe higher prices (especially of essentials) are not necessarily a symptom of inflation, but rather a convenient way for the planners to transfer some of the public's excess purchasing power into the state treasury. With the potential inflationary pressure of pent-up demand as the main headache in the early stages of economic reform, there is a natural, strong

[6] This change in the traditional housing policy does not imply any substantial increase in the supply of apartments, the construction of which is still to be limited by the allocation of building materials. The only change is in the principles of financing: people will have to spend a larger proportion of their incomes for housing, leaving less for other purposes. Thus it is purely a deflationary move. While private pocketbooks will not bear the entire cost of new housing construction, the higher rates and down payments will absorb a substantial amount of potential purchasing power.

temptation to take an easy way out and decree a price increase for some selected types of goods and services. Every little bit helps and apart from housing, this device has already been applied, among others, to subsidized factory canteen meals, to transportation and cost, and to various forms of entertainment.

In Hungary substantial price increases were decreed by the central planners even prior to the adoption of a definite reform program (but in obvious preparation for it). As of February 1, 1966, there was a 25 to 50 per cent hike in the prices of pork, beef, and other meat products, as well as of bread, grains and dairy products (except for milk) (103). This required an upward readjustment of restaurant and canteen prices. On April 1966 the cost of fuel went up (124). Coal prices were increased by 25 per cent and the charges for central heating were raised by the same amount. Finally, as of June 1, 1966, Hungarians were paying 100 per cent more for municipal transportation. In Poland too, prices of coal, gas, and electricity were increased as early as in April 1963 (178) and some other price adjustments, including those for such staples as cigarettes, were made subsequently (182).

There has been some upward movement of wages too. But the general policy seems to be one of restricting the overall growth of real incomes, while at the same time increasing the nominal earnings of certain categories of workers. Wages are to rise but at a much slower rate than the cost of living. Thus at least a part of the cost of economic reform is being passed on to the population (especially to unskilled wage earners and salaried employees).[7]

The effects of reform on wages are likely to be much more complex than this. In principle the introduction of a more flexible system of indirect controls should tend to increase the earnings of the more productive workers. This, however, would apply only to factory workers, miners, and some transport employees (in sectors where productivity per worker can be effectively measured and directly attributed) (51). It leaves out the great mass of state and municipal employees in such "non-productive" occupations as retail trade, health services, education, public

---

7 "ir," "The Relationship of Wages and the Cost of Living," *Zemedelske Noviny* (December 23, 1966).

transportation, etc., as well as the huge apparatus of economic bureaucracy. All these workers face the prospect of higher living costs without any off-setting hope of increased earnings (24). No doubt something will be done for them. There may be wage and salary increases for selected categories (as in Poland and Bulgaria), or a substantial increase in family allowances (as in Hungary). But on the whole these "non-productive" workers, together with the unemployed, are likely to bear much of the cost of economic reform.

Altogether, there is a conspicuous lack of any comprehensive, across-the-board wage reform proposals in the "new model" blueprints. While the prices of raw materials, energy, capital, and finished products are to be brought up gradually to their true economic level (37), human labor will apparently continue to be underpaid. This is the case not only in countries with a substantial manpower surplus (where workers might be expected to have less bargaining power) but also in those where labor is in short supply. Thus even though the classic Marxist slogan "to each according to his need" has been modified to read "to each according to his productive performance," the monetary value of this performance is still to be determined by the state planners (except, perhaps, in Czechoslovakia).[8]

The purpose of this wage restraint is apparently to contain the inflationary pressures in the economy. But even in those countries where enterprise managers will have some leeway to adjust wages upward, the financial means available for this purpose will be quite limited. At best, the enterprise director's right to determine either wages or the number of workers employed is limited a) by the size of the enterprise wage fund (i.e., total planned value of labor costs) which is still to be centrally controlled, and b) by various prior claims of the state treasury (such as interest charges on capital) which have to be paid regardless of operational profits. Moreover, there are indications that the trade unions may oppose changes in wage rates which would provide greater differentials for skilled workers.[9]

---

[8] Ibid.

[9] In Czechoslovakia strikes have been threatened if wage differential proposals would be put into effect. Cf. J. Kanturek's article in *Kulturni Tvorba* (May 26, 1966).

The situation is even more complex in Bulgaria where a modified "residual claimant" wage system is to be introduced. Under this system the worker will receive both the guaranteed and incentive payments only after all other claims on enterprise earnings have been paid (4). In an extreme case of an inefficient establishment, this may mean that wage earners will be worse off than before the reform, when wages were paid regardless of the performance of the factory. Under the "residual claimant" scheme only a portion of the earnings—80 to 90 per cent of the state-determined wage rates (but not of higher wage scales granted above this minimum by the enterprise director)—are to be fully guaranteed (256). If the enterprise cannot pay the rest, it has to borrow money from the bank. However, even before an enterprise pays the guaranteed part of its wage bill it must use its general revenue to cover a multitude of other claims: depreciation, raw materials, interest on various capital funds, fines and penalties, taxes and compulsory payments into various enterprise, and "trust" funds including the reserve, development, and social consumption funds. If in addition, the enterprise must pay interest on bank credits which were used to cover deficits from the previous year, the worker's claim may be residual indeed. In effect, the workers are being asked to guarantee their own income out of future earnings of their enterprise.

Similarly, the proposals to use profit sharing as an incentive may fall to the ground in at least two ways. First, if an enterprise wishes to direct a larger share of its receipts to raising wages, its income may be subject to almost confiscatory tax rates. Second, the authorities can effectively discourage the enterprise from raising wage rates by 1) requiring a larger contribution to the various enterprise or "trust" funds, 2) increasing levies on capital, 3) raising the turnover tax, and 4) increasing depreciation rates. In short, the central planners can still effectively block increases in wages if they wish.

Thus the inevitable rise in the cost of living is not likely to be offset by increases in earnings—a fact which accounts for the notoriously suspicious attitude of the workers in Eastern Europe toward economic reforms (115). Their anxiety is now beginning to be reflected in the attitude of the party-run trade unions. At the meeting of the presidium of Hungarian Trade Unions in

February 1966, demands were voiced that henceforth earnings should keep pace with price increases (123). Strong fears were also expressed that the implementation of the new economic model would lead to mass dismissals.

Another price of reform which may bear heavily upon thousands of workers is the closing down of inefficient enterprises. Some of these enterprises are huge industrial status symbols constructed during the Stalin era, and they are maintained in operation only because the state covers their deficits. The authorities must now decide whether to close them down or to find some way of salvaging them. (This may be one of the real motives behind the much-publicized Soviet and other East European deals with Western automobile manufacturers to establish production of Fiats, Renaults, etc., under license.) But apart from the "status symbols" there remain hundreds of small unprofitable enterprises which cannot expect to weather any thoroughgoing economic reform. So far this matter has been seriously tackled only in Czechoslovakia. There the authorities have long ago reached the conclusion that the subsidizing of unprofitable factories is a luxury which the Czechoslovak economy cannot afford. Some 1,300 were liquidated during 1964–65 and during the current five-year plan (1966–70) another 1,400 inefficient enterprises are scheduled to close down with a loss of 60,000 jobs (26).

Apart from the general problem of uneconomic and unprofitable undertakings, certain branches of industry are likely to be particularly hit by the economic efficiency drive. This is, for instance, the case in the coal mining industry. Here the world-wide switch-over from coal to more economic oil as the source of energy has coincided in time with the need to close the mines, which were unprofitable to start with. This problem is especially acute in Hungary where some 20,000 miners must soon be laid off, according to official estimates.[10] The question of what to do with the surplus manpower in the mines was discussed at the Ninth Party Congress (November–December 1966) but no concrete measures were proposed, although Kadar himself said that

[10] Report of the Minister of Heavy Industry, F. Levardi, as published in *Nepszabadsag* (December 31, 1966). Radio Kossuth (Budapest) in its broadcast of February 8, 1967 gave an even higher figure of 23,000 miners to be laid off.

this problem had to be solved "fairly honestly and according to humanitarian principles" (132). Early in 1967 the Ministries of Heavy Industry and Labor drafted jointly some regulations which are meant to facilitate the transfer of surplus labor from the coal mines to other branches of industry (128). These include extensive retraining schemes and special benefits to cover the costs of transfer. It is also recognized, however, that the bulk of older miners (who may be the first to go) are beyond the retraining age and these are to be paid "a lump sum" as a compensation. The exact amount of this lump sum is to be determined by the enterprise manager "on the grounds of his personal judgement." This is hardly the "fair and humanitarian" approach of which Kadar spoke at the congress.

But the real problem is that in Hungary, as in Czechoslovakia (and in other Moscow bloc countries as well), many thousands of workers and employees are about to lose their jobs as the result of the closing down of uneconomic and unprofitable enterprises.[11]

What is to be done with these workers? In May 1966 this problem was discussed by the Czechoslovak Trade Union Council, and the final resolution suggested that workers facing dismissal be given retraining courses along with "social payments" (unemployment benefits) during their period of joblessness (36). The problem bulks large, both politically and economically, in a country where the very word unemployment is taboo. So far, the closing of unprofitable enterprises in Czechoslovakia is estimated to have cost 35,000 jobs (26), and this may be only the beginning. Commenting on the trade union discussions, one observer suggested that if the principle of liquidating unprofitable factories were to be applied rigorously, it would be necessary to close 10 per cent of the existing industrial enterprises.[12]

This is all a part of an even broader issue. For in actual fact there is no difference between the problem of those workers who shall lose jobs because of the closing down of unprofitable enterprises and those who shall join the ranks of the unemployed as a result of the natural tendency on the part of the managements

[11] The problem of the closing down of uneconomic undertakings is already discussed in the Soviet Union (see 211).

[12] A commentary by Bozena Kubinova broadcast by Radio Prague on May 6, 1966.

of other factories to cut their labor costs. In both cases we are dealing with an attempt to correct the errors of the past period, which promoted the excessive growth of employment and indiscriminate use of resources. But it is also obvious that those dismissed from work should not bear the economic and social consequences of the mistaken policy pursued for years by the party elite.

What we are dealing with here is an ostensible contradiction between requirements of economic rationalization and the social and economic interest of large social groups. But the real issue is that the rationalization measures should be treated in a more sophisticated way. For, from the point of view of the economy as a whole, an unprofitable factory is as negative a phenomenon as the growth of unemployment. And therefore before an unprofitable factory is closed it is necessary to make proper arrangements to ensure employment for the dismissed workers and employees.

It should be stressed that the suggestions put forward by the Federation of Czechoslovak Trade Unions were along those very lines. The remedies suggested include both the retraining of the dismissed workers at the expense of the state as well as safeguarding the economic needs of their families during the period of the temporary unemployment by introduction of unemployment benefits. In order to avoid the unpleasant word "unemployment," trade union resolution calls them "social payments" (65). Czechoslovak trade unions have also appealed to the workers to show their understanding for the need to close unprofitable factories, assuring them of every assistance in finding new jobs corresponding to their skill and capabilities.

Thus, whichever way one looks at the problem, the social and economic cost of the reforms have to be measured in terms of increased unemployment and a fall in living standards. Such is the price which has to be paid for years of mismanagement and idolatry of abstract dogmas. This, however, does not change the basic point that the reforms are absolutely necessary and a positive step in the right direction. The negative features described above are the inevitable short-term effects of the process of rationalization. In the longer run, all these dislocations are likely to disappear, as the economies concerned evolve a new dynamics of growth based this time on closer relationship between production and the market. But in the meantime the fears and apprehensions of the working class (which is bound to bear the main burden of those costs) have generated a powerful pressure for a reappraisal of the role of trade unions.

8

★

TRADE UNIONS: AN AGONIZING REAPPRAISAL

Trade unions as we know them in the West have no place in the structure of a communist society. The basic doctrine of Marxism-Leninism prescribes that at the stage of "socialism" all political, economic, and social activity must be regulated and controlled by the vanguard of the proletariat, i.e., the communist party. The people as a whole and even large groups within the proletariat itself are incapable of creating the new order. The working class must be guided by the party along a strictly regimented path toward the ultimate goal of communism.

There is thus no room for a mass organization of industrial workers such as a trade union, except as a purely subordinate body to assist the party in achieving its economic and social objectives. By definition those objectives are set by the "vanguard of the proletariat" and embody the aims and aspirations of the working class as a whole; there is thus no theoretical need to promote the particular interests of the organized workers. And since all the means of production belong in theory to the people and are run on their behalf by the communist party, there is no room for a conflict of interest between management and labor.

From these myths came the stalinist concept of the trade union as a "transmission belt" for the implementation of party directives in the economic sector. The main task of the unions was the so-called "struggle for production," in accordance with the thesis that the standard of living of the working masses can rise only in direct relationship to the volume of goods produced. Since there were no capitalists, ran the theory, the higher the industrial output the more goods would be distributed among the workers.

Although this traditional Marxist concept of the trade union has long been out of touch with reality, the party authorities still adhere stubbornly to the doctrine of "unity of interests." As late as July 1966 the theoretical monthly of the Hungarian communist party flatly declared: "The basic point is that in our system the interests of the trade unions and the interests of the state are identical" (125).

Yet economic reality can no longer be hidden behind outdated dogma, however categorically stated and however oft repeated. The introduction of the new economic model has brought into focus the eternal problem of relations between management and labor. One of the basic effects of the economic reforms now being implemented throughout the Soviet bloc is to separate the party from industrial management, at least on the enterprise level. Under the new system the decision-making process is being decentralized and individual enterprise directors are gradually gaining greater autonomy and wider prerogatives. At the same time, a new class of professional managers is coming into being. The old type of enterprise director—the classic party hack— is gradually being replaced by a new man: a fully qualified "socialist entrepreneur."[1]

Thus the new economic model has created a completely new situation, at least within the enterprises. The decentralization of economic decision making has considerably increased the prerogatives of factory managers. At the same time, the introduction of profit as the basic yardstick of economic efficiency has given the managers powerful incentive to seek better economic results. In this their immediate interests will not necessarily be the same as those of the workers. A situation has arisen in which the greater part of the inevitable economic and social costs of economic reform may well have to be borne primarily by the working class.[2] In the process the conflict of interest between the managers responsible for the economic effectiveness of individual enterprises and the working masses is becoming far more open and acute.

As a result the workers have a natural desire to create an effective counterweight to the growing economic strength and political importance of the managerial class. Simultaneously, there arises

[1] This problem is discussed at length in Chapter 6.

[2] See Chapter 7.

an obvious need for machinery to carry the workers' postulates both to the enterprise managers and to the state and party authorities—the need to create an institution that genuinely represents the workers' interests (118).

In Yugoslavia an attempt is now being made to solve the new antagonism between labor and management by promoting the concept of workers' self-management. This concept emphasizes the role of the workers as co-producers and neatly sidesteps the basic issues involved in reestablishing genuinely independent trade unions. It is still an open question in Yugoslavia whether or not the workers' councils will ultimately develop into a true representation of workingclass interests and eventually supersede the existing trade union organization. However, elsewhere in Eastern Europe the party elite has stubbornly opposed the growth of workers' councils. When such councils sprang up ten years ago on the crest of the revolutionary wave in Poland and in Hungary, they were subsequently deprived of any real power.[3]

As the economic reforms move ahead they will open up new possibilities and raise new challenges for the existing trade unions. As enterprises seek to maximize their profits they will inevitably want to lower their production costs—including their wage bills. Moreover, the inevitable rise in prices resulting from the rational use of economic resources can also have a strong negative effect on living standards. The closing down of unprofitable factories or production lines may increase unemployment; someone must fight to assure these unemployed a minimum livelihood and to establish facilities for retraining them and finding them new jobs. Hundreds of problems will arise in the transition to the new economic system that are within the sphere of trade union activity.[4]

At the same time trade union officials in some of the communist countries are showing awareness of the need for change. A market economy will not need "transmission belts" for its basic operating instrument is to be material incentive. Moreover, it is one thing for the union officials to identify themselves with party decisions

---

[3] In Hungary, workers' councils disappeared after the 1956 revolution. In Poland they survived until 1958 when they were merged with the party and trade union organizations into the so-called "workers' self-government conferences."

[4] This point has been emphasized at a special meeting of Czech trade unions (see 36).

and press for their implementation but quite another to play the role of supervisors on behalf of the managerial class (131). And this is what would happen if they were to keep on with the old-fashioned "struggle for production" under the new conditions. This is why many trade union officials are anxious to redefine the tasks of their unions. They want to dust off their role as protectors of the rights and interests of the workers, a role that has always existed on paper but has been completely neglected in practice and deemphasized in theory.

Finally, implementation of the new economic system also creates a new situation for the party. Until now the party has been identified with all economic decisions, from the most fundamental down to the least significant. Inevitably, it has borne the odium of any unpopular measure. The new situation gives the party an opportunity to shift responsibility for the conflict between employer and employee down to the level of enterprise managers and local trade unions. The communist leadership would cease to be blamed for many unpopular economic decisions. What is equally important, it would no longer be directly involved in labor conflicts at the enterprise level and might even in time assume the role of impartial arbiter. The political advantages to be derived from such a disengagement are obvious, and the more intelligent members of the party elite are bound to grasp the possibilities.

Such is the climate of change created by the economic reforms. Now let us see what has actually been happening within the trade union movement throughout Eastern Europe. The initial response has been slow and tentative, for several reasons. First of all, neither the party nor the top trade union officials are yet ready to abandon the old doctrine of "unity of interests" (106). Neither do they want to concede that a mass organization other than the party can represent the aims and aspirations of the working class. Finally, their preoccupation with the need to rationalize the economy has left little time for considering the inevitable social and political side effects.

Thus the question of labor-management relations within the framework of the new economic system has been virtually ignored. Some lip service was paid to the need to reappraise and expand the role of the trade unions, but no East European communist party has seriously come to grips with the problem, either in theory or practice.

Although party authorities have neglected the issue, the trade union officials have found themselves under increasing pressure from the rank and file. This is particularly true in Hungary where the Kadar regime made the political mistake of ordering a round of price increases even before the economic reforms had been given their first approval by the Central Committee.[5] Moreover, the Hungarian scheme, unlike the other East European blueprints, does not interpose any medium-level organizational structure between the enterprises and the ministries. Thus the questions of working conditions and pay were by and large left up to the factory directors. The shock of unexpected price increases combined with the workers' fear of excessive prerogatives for individual managers resulted in a widespread demand for a change in the character of the Hungarian trade union movement (123).

Partially in response to this pressure from below, the Hungarian Council of Ministers and the Presidium of the Trade Union Council worked out a joint resolution in mid-June 1966. As explained by Sandor Gaspar, head of the TUC, future relations between the communist state and the trade unions are to be based on the premise "that in the course of building socialism, the trade union movement becomes the true representative of the organized workers and that (the movement) may take an independent position in all fields of economic, social and cultural life" (129). The trade unions, argued Gaspar, must acquire a deeper knowledge of the opinions, aspirations, and viewpoints of their rank and file membership and must explain these attitudes to the party authorities.

Gaspar also acknowledged that in certain cases the interests of the organized workers might be different from the interests of the socialist state. "I such a conflict should arise, and if the disputed issue could not be settled by subsequent consultations, the trade union would have a right to publicize its differing view." He added that this "would constitute a completely new feature in trade union work."

This recognition of the right to dissent, tentative and ambiguous

---

[5] See Chapter 4.

though it may be, must be seen as the first step toward recognizing the possible conflict of interest between management and labor. Another step in that direction is the gradual disengagement of Hungarian trade unions from their quasi-managerial functions. "The present practice, which allows the trade union committees to interfere with the manager's work, must be abandoned," Gaspar declared in his *Nepszabadsag* interview. He spoke out in favor of reducing the number of issues on which factory managers cannot make a binding decision without the agreement of trade unions and intimated that the unions would fully support the principle of "one-man management" in exchange for greater autonomy in their own sphere.

The first real attempt to redefine the role of Hungarian trade unions was made in an unsigned editorial published in the July 1966 issue of *Partelet*, an Hungarian communist party monthly. Although the article reaffirmed the principle of the "unity of interest," it also acknowledged that protection of workers' rights is a principal, if not the only, function of the unions:

> The trade unions take a comprehensive part in socialist construction. While assuming responsibility (for this construction), they take part in the shaping of economic tasks, organize the workers and raise a protest against irregularities. In this way they are able to protect the interests of the working class and the organized workers, and to promote the desire to increase wealth and culture, as well as to improve labor conditions.
>
> The Party expects from the trade unions more courageous and independent initiative in their constructive work in the protection of workers' interests, as well as a more effective participation in the realization of their objectives. (125)

One can detect here a subtle shift of emphasis from the former paramount task—the "struggle for production"—to the more traditional trade union duty of "protecting the workers' interests." More significantly, the article in *Partelet* went on to pronounce a partial separation of the party and the unions: "It follows that the Party guides the trade unions ideologically and politically, but not by organizational means. Party officials and individual cells do not interfere in the everyday activities of the unions." Thus the old relationship of subordination is apparently to be replaced by a new principle of cooperation between the two (still unequal) partners.

The *Partelet* article also recognized "the greater possibility of differences of opinion" arising from enlarged trade union authority and independence. But it stressed that the unions should not only "clarify the reasons for a difference of opinion," but also do their best to "reconcile and settle those differences, in cooperation" with appropriate state authorities. In plain language this means seeking a compromise between the opposing views.

Behind all the dialectical arguments of *Partelet* one can detect a subtle retreat. In any future clash between organized labor on one side and state authorities and industrial bureaucrats on the other, the authorities will not be in a position to impose their will; they must work toward compromise.

The Gaspar interview and the article in *Partelet* were tentative first steps toward greater autonomy for Hungarian trade unions; but these statements were still permeated with the old spirit of solidarism. To the party leaders the main tasks of the unions are to advise and reconcile rather than oppose. This is hardly consistent with the organized workers' demands for an effective counterweight to the managers' growing power and for an institution able to press their particular postulates. This was indicated at the August 1966 meeting of the National Council of Trade Unions where it was admitted that a great number of complaints were arriving at the trade union headquarters—most of them over price increases, others over living standards in general (116). Workers also complained about the inhuman attitude of certain managers. Even Sandor Gaspar, a ranking member of the Politburo, thought it necessary to emphasize that the trade unions were seriously concerned about "spontaneous and unwarranted" increases in consumer prices. He warned his party associates that "this may have several harmful consequences" (105).

Gaspar set forth his views at length in the September 1966 issue of the party's theoretical monthly, *Tarsadalmi Szemle* (126). First he emphasized that the unions intended to make a clean break with the stalinist past.

This dogmatic and sectarian political attitude (in the past) deprived the trade union movement of its historic basic function, its life and soul: the representation and the safeguarding of the workers' interests —quite apart from any consideration that, even under socialist conditions, the individual interest of the employee and overall social interests may be in conflict. *As a result of uncertain and inadequate assertion of those interests, the masses lost their confidence in trade unions.* [italics added]

Within the framework of the New Economic Model, wrote Gaspar, there must be a concurrent increase in the prerogatives of the enterprise managers and in the rights and duties of the trade unions. The unions would have a twin task: they must "guarantee the workers the most favorable development of their living and working conditions, their labor rights, their wages and incomes" and "improvement of their social benefits"; they must also fight against violators of the labor law and against bureaucratic abuses.

Gaspar was far more specific on the second or defensive task, since it pertained to trade union activities on the enterprise level where the growing managerial prerogatives must inevitably be matched by greater union freedom of action. But he could offer only vague generalities on wage and price determination, since those are overall problems in the domain of the central planners. Gaspar kept repeating that "trade unions are an independent and non-Party organization" and that union functionaries have a duty to evaluate economic developments "from a specific trade union point of view." But he would say no more than that trade unions must be "consulted" before any economic move affecting their membership is made. In an extreme "controversy" the union might "publicize" its divergent views.

Still vaguer was the definition of trade unions' new tasks put forward by Sandor Beckl, one of the secretaries of the Trade Union Council, in the August 1966 issue of the unions' own monthly *Munka*. Beckl declared that in the new economic system trade unions should "participate collectively in the management and control of the economy." Their task would be "to represent the collective and individual interests of the workers and to adapt those interests to state and social interest." He also spoke of the need to increase the rights of the unions and of their duty to "fight for the satisfaction of realistic economic, cultural and social demands of the workers" (97).

The use of the word "realistic" implied that the final decision would be made by the state-employer, as represented by the central planners (who will determine the "realism" of union demands). It also indicated that union leadership in Hungary was lagging behind the prevailing mood of its rank and file members. Indeed, Beckl was forced to admit at a plenary meeting of the Trade Union Council at the end of September that no final decision had yet been reached on the role of the unions. But he predicted confidently that "trade unions would secure for the workers more say in economic management" (127).

It is precisely in the sphere of management, however, that the party leadership in Hungary seems unwilling to tolerate union interference. Rezsö Nyers, the architect of the Hungarian economic reform, has argued rather emphatically that "state enterprises are not built in the principle of self-administration"; neither workers nor unions ought to participate in selecting the enterprise director or in the actual management (114):

> Under the principle of one-man leadership, state enterprises are led by managers appointed by the state and the direction of production and trade processes is the sole prerogative of the managers. Managers do not share their spheres of authority and responsibility in such matters with local trade unions.

The unions according to Nyers merely have the right to participate in the newly created "supervising committees" (the composition of which is still rather unclear) "in order that they may have a concrete opportunity for exercising their control tasks" on behalf of the workers they represent. From Nyers' arguments it follows that the activities of Hungarian trade unions are to be confined strictly to safeguarding workers' interests and to matters directly involving living and working conditions. Even here their prerogatives are quite limited. Nyers made it clear that in such matters the right to decide still rests with the enterprise manager (and the central planners), although they must consult with the trade unions. This might be called at most a right of limited co-determination.

Nevertheless, even this restricted scope of activity will call for some reorganization of trade union structure, as well as for a basic change in the mentality of trade union officials. This latter point was underlined repeatedly by Tivadar Nemeslaki, General Secretary of the Hungarian Steel and Metal Workers Trade Union. He said in an interview, published in *Nepszabadsag*, that the basic present need was for a completely new attitude on the part of shop stewards and other trade union officials in the enterprises (131). He advised them not to behave as functionaries but "to talk with a worker's tongue." Nemeslaki also said that trade union activists in enterprises must become more and more conscious "of the mood, troubles and problems" of their members and urged shop stewards to

> represent the interest of the workers in a courageous way. They should expose various conflicts of interest, as well as contradictions, because only thus will it be possible to eliminate and solve them in the interest of society. Experience has shown that subordinating the trade union stewards hampers the courageous espousal and consistent representation of their fellow workers' interests.

Such a change in outlook and mentality may perhaps be helped by reorganizational measures giving more authority to the trade unions at the enterprise level. Some of the forthcoming changes were discussed by Gabor Somosköi, another secretary of the Trade Union Council, in October 1966. Somosköi admitted frankly that higher trade union organs did not give adequate support to local union officials in the past, and promised that this will be remedied. He also disclosed that changes in the existing organizational structure of the unions are in the offing (117).

The first such change will be at the level of individual enterprises employing 300 or more workers. The party's factory councils will be eliminated and their functions assumed by newly-created factory trade union councils which will also have the responsibility for certain new tasks. The councils, of 50–80 members, will elect enterprise committees. The committees will be concerned with specific day-to-day problems such as workers' grievances, while more important matters like the distribution of profits will be handled by the union councils.

The second reorganizational measure, which concerns only a few industrial trade unions, will be carried out in large national enterprises covering a whole branch of industry (cement and chalk or beer, etc.), where an enterprise council will replace the present executive committees. This body will coordinate all trade unions in the enterprise's factory units. The enterprise trade union council will elect enterprise committees to direct the work of the factory councils and committees. Although this switch to the industrial-branch principle will be limited at first, Somosköi said that even in the national enterprises affected, "the maintenance and operation of regional and county union bodies might still be necessary."

All this still did not explain in what matters the trade unions would have the right of decision, opinion, control or veto. But at the Ninth Party Congress in November 1966, several speakers were more explicit. Sandor Gaspar declared that the unions would have more to say in questions of workers' living conditions. They would also have the right to veto managerial acts that violated "laws and collective agreements" (106). Party chief Kadar promised that the unions would take part "in the activities and management of enterprises so they will feel responsible for the entire work of the firm"; he also said they would play "a role in the evaluation, affirmation and dismissal of plant managers" (133).

The veto right was discussed more fully in a provincial newspaper *Bekes Megyei Nepujsag* on December 11, 1966. The paper said that in the future the veto right will be used by enterprise, regional, or industrial trade unions if "the plant or other economic leaders violate legal measures or important mutual agreements such as collective agreements, the rules of socialist coexistence or behavior expected from socialist leaders."

> The veto can be filed by the trade union organ—the TU committee as a body, for instance—but not by the TU committee secretary or other TU members. Why? To exercise a veto should be an extraordinary measure; personal and individual motives for a veto can thus be eliminated. The manager affected will be informed of the union's displeasure either orally or in writing, but the veto itself, adequately documented, must be filed in writing immediately with the proper economic and union authorities. After the veto the managers cannot enforce their orders until the superior economic and trade union bodies reach a decision. The manager of the enterprise can appeal the veto within two days and lodge a protest within eight days with his superior. (108)

I have reviewed at length the developments within the trade union movement in Hungary, because they are as yet the most symptomatic and the most characteristic example of the impact which the introduction of a new economic system is having on the stereotyped trade union institutions and attitudes which date back to Stalin's era. Both the specifics of the new Hungarian economic model and the serious political errors committed by the Kadar regime combined here to speed up the institutional changes, which were inevitable anyway. And although Hungary is at present well ahead of the rest of the Moscow bloc, as far as the process of reassessment of the future tasks of trade unions is concerned, the logic of the new economic system is bound to promote a similar qualitative change in the other trade union movements of Eastern Europe.

In Czechoslovakia, where the problem of matching greater authority of enterprise managers with greater independence for the trade unions is perhaps as acute as in Hungary, the official attitude has been rather hesitant and contradictory. As late as June 1966 the resolution of the 13th Party Congress had, in essence, reaffirmed the traditional "transmission belt" concept of the unions. In enumerating the unions' basic tasks it put "political-educational work toward securing greater productive efficiency" far ahead of the "care of workers' needs and interests" (80). The party leadership still stresses from time to time the dogmatic view that "the interests of the socialist state and the interests of the working people are identical" (73).

There are signs, however, that the union officials themselves are trying to show some independence and to carve out a greater margin of autonomy for themselves. Miroslav Pastyrik, Chairman of the Trade Union Council, declared at the 13th Party Congress that "trade unions must always keep their own face as an independent and voluntary organization" (79). The Central Trade Union Council emphasized a few months earlier that its basic task was to ensure that the rightful demands of the workers were satisfied (78), while at the Trade Union Congress, Pastyrik called for a "broader incorporation of workers in preparing the plans of individual enterprises" (83).

This was not just verbal image-building. Although far less assertive than Hungarian unions in discussing their role in the new economic model, the Czechoslovak unions have taken an independent stand more than once when the vital interests of their members were at stake. The union representatives who helped draw up the new labor code (effective January 1, 1966) managed to introduce a provision that makes unemployment benefits possible. On that basis the government reportedly agreed in December 1966 to measures providing unemployment benefits and other forms of support for displaced workers (69). On the local level, one union made a successful demand to stop production in an enamel factory in Filakovo in central Slovakia because of appalling industrial safety conditions (68). The unions have also been self-critical of their stalinist past, although less frankly and definitely than in Hungary. Nevertheless, the article in question concluded that "the mistakes of the past do show the need for a greater autonomy of the trade union movement" (31).

Several articles have also appeared dealing with the role of the unions in the new economic system. One of them indicated that considerable pressure has been put upon union officials for more active protection of workers' interests.

> The following point of view is often expressed: What do the unions actually do for the workers (apart from distributing vouchers for recreation centers), how do they defend the workers' interests? What do they do about certain problems they should handle? (54)

The article's answers were rather indefinite, confined to generalities about workers' participation in the process of management "through their elected union representatives." The unions were said to have the right of co-decision, but in respect to social rather than economic questions.

All in all, the issue of the unions' role in the new economic system does not seem to have received adequate attention in Czechoslovakia, probably because of a preoccupation with the more pressing problems of economic efficiency. However, discussion of the problem has picked up since the beginning of 1967. In any case, party leaders would be naïve if they believed, in the words of the article cited above, that "trade unions must convince the workers that . . . they are their own organization, capable of backing them when they are in the right, but also of rejecting their opinions when they are wrong and convincing them of the necessity of unpleasant alternatives when the interests of the whole society are involved" (54).

The situation elsewhere in the bloc is even more obscure. In the Soviet Union the leading economic reformers do seem to realize that the unions' power will have to be increased, because enterprise managers are now to have a direct say in determining premiums and bonuses—an integral part of their workers' pay packet. Professor Liberman was certainly explicit on this point in an interview with the Czechoslovak trade union daily *Prace.* He insisted that "the role of trade unions will grow considerably, for they must be given more rights—not only in the legal but also in the economic sense. . . . The unions have to play a decisive role in the question of economic incentives" (66). On the other hand, *Trud,* the Soviet trade union organ, has emphasized that the main task is still "the struggle for production and the problems of work discipline" (219).

East Germany is still farther behind. A definite attempt has been made there to limit the unions' freedom of action at the enterprise level by subjecting them to strict supervision by the Kreis (district) authorities. In accordance with the prevailing industrial structure, the main emphasis is put on the unions' role at the trust (VVB) level, which is the new center of economic power. But even here the unions are being asked to preserve their traditional role as an instrument of management since "their main energy must be concentrated on tasks arising from the need to fulfill the national plan [and] . . . on making suggestions to that effect to the general directors of the VVB's."[5]

A very peculiar situation has developed in Yugoslavia, where the unions apparently are quite willing to forgo their traditional functions at the enterprise level while trying to establish their power on the national level. Svetozar Vukmanovic-Tempo, the national head of the unions, argued that their role in Yugoslavia must necessarily be different from that of trade unions in a capitalist society or those unions that function under conditions of state capitalism in other communist countries.[6] There is no need to represent the specific interests of the employees on the enterprise level, he maintains, since all factories in Yugoslavia are "social

[5] Unsigned article, *Tribüne* (June 11, 1966).

[6] Vukmanovic-Tempo ceased to be the Chairman of Yugoslav Trade Unions early in 1967. His resignation was reported in *Borba* (February 22, 1967).

property" managed by the workers themselves. Thus there can be no labor-management conflict in the accepted sense (240).

But none of this excludes a conflict between the unions and the central authorities over concrete economic measures affecting organized workers:

Disagreement may well arise between the trade unions and the state administration, but it will not be disagreement on the construction of a socialist society but a disagreement on particular concrete matters—which can be answered only in practice. (240)

Vukmanovic-Tempo holds that the unions should have a "decisive function" in determining their members' personal income when it is affected by taxes and other instruments of state economic policy. In doing so they "cannot act as ordinary executors of a fixed planned policy, but must strive to have their point of view adopted by the state administration."

Vukmanovic-Tempo's claim that the Yugoslav system of workers' self-government eliminates all labor-management conflicts in the enterprises seems, at best, exaggerated and premature. There were 504 strikes, involving some 20,000 workers, in Yugoslavia during 1964 and 1965 (229). Although the official atitude is that there "were not strikes in the classic meaning of the word" but merely "protest work stoppages," the causes enumerated by *Borba* are typical of industrial disputes elsewhere. Low earnings, arbitrary increases in piece-work rates, the uncompromising attitude of management officials, and bad working conditions were all listed by the Belgrade daily as the most frequent reasons for work stoppages.

Paradoxically, the Yugoslav party sees the situation in a slightly different light than the trade union leadership does. In April 1964 Tito himself encouraged the workers "to put pressure" both on the government and on management to protect their rights (246). Moreover, it was agreed in principle that strikes are not harmful and not illegal (241). This indicated both a political and an ideological reorientation toward industrial conflicts. The Yugoslav communists may still maintain that a particular work stoppage is merely a warning signal, but they really consider the strike "a weapon directed primarily against economic bureaucracy" (234, 238). (The economic bureaucracy is in some ways a rival political group, which may well explain the benevolent attitude of the

Yugoslav party toward "work stoppages.") But Yugoslav unions are also interested in using workers' protests as a lever to obtain a greater say in state economic policy. In November 1966 Vukmanovic-Tempo spoke to a group of miners on the crisis in the coal industry. He attacked the policy of closing coal mines and laying off workers, and called on the miners "to organize themselves to influence state policy." Blaming the coal crisis on "mistaken planning," he demanded that the state set up a special fund to help displaced miners (231).[7]

Yugoslavia is in some ways an exceptional case. One must assume that the trend in Hungary is more characteristic of future developments in Eastern Europe. The Yugoslavs have chosen the path of workers' self-government with all that this concept implies, but the other countries seem firmly committed to the "one-man management" principle. This means that managerial prerogatives are bound to grow with the gradual implementation of the new economic model. The more freedom of action managers get, the greater will be the need for employees to defend their own interests. Genuine reform is bound to result in the expression of these conflicts. For the unions it is both an opportunity and a challenge: they must either return to their original role or be replaced by new institutions that will give the workers genuine representation.

---

[7] A much longer text of Vukmanovic's speech was broadcast by Radio Zagreb on October 11, 1966.

9

★

REFORMS IN AGRICULTURE

The economic reforms in Eastern Europe began in industry and trade. But there are good reasons, political and economic, why they are now being extended to farming as well. No economy can maintain a *dirigiste* system in one sector and attempt to introduce quasi-market conditions in the others. No dictatorship without a permanent apparatus of terror can exploit the peasants indefinitely the way they were exploited under Stalin. No social class would passively submit to this kind of economic discrimination, and the peasants, who still constitute about half of the population of Eastern Europe, are very conscious of their numerical strength.

Aside from politics, there are valid practical economic reasons for applying the new principles to agriculture. Most of Eastern Europe has a serious farm problem (except perhaps for Poland and Rumania, where for various reasons it is not as urgent). The basic symptoms of the trouble are the same everywhere. The output of grain has been stagnating and periodically a bad harvest shakes a country's whole economy; it means a shortage of bread and fodder, leading to a decline in meat production and the expenditure of foreign exchange on grain imports, which in turn plays havoc with the balance of payments.

Agricultural output as a whole has been anything but dynamic. The indices of net production compiled by the US Department of Agriculture (see Table 2 below) show that in 1965 output per capita for the Soviet bloc as a whole was about what it had been five years before. The bloc as a whole suffered a sharp setback in this period, mainly because of the poor grain harvests in the Soviet Union, which normally accounts for over half the aggregate output. The per capita index of output is a particularly meaningful measure of real progress in farm production because it takes account of population growth. Per capita output in the bloc dropped some 5 per cent in 1965 and went back almost to the 1960 level. The bumper crops of 1966 brought about a temporary relief, but did not change the basic issue of the low productivity of state and cooperative farms and the pressure on foreign exchange reserves, resulting from grain imports.

The overall stagnation of East European agriculture is well illustrated by the following table (255).[1]

TABLE 2.
USSR AND EASTERN EUROPE: INDICES OF NET AGRICULTURAL PRODUCTION, TOTAL AND PER CAPITA, BY COUNTRY
(1957–59 = 100)

	Total Output					*Per Capital Output*			
COUNTRY	1960	1961	1963	1964	1965	1960	1963	1964	1965
USSR	101	107	101	117	109	97	93	106	98
East Europe:									
Poland	109	120	118	118	122	106	110	109	111
GDR	112	85	98	102	103	113	100	104	103
CSSR	102	99	104	106	94	102	101	103	94
Hungary	104	97	104	105	106	103	102	104	103
Rumania	108	116	110	116	121	106	106	110	114
Bulgaria	109	104	111	118	118	106	106	112	111
Yugoslavia	102	99	111	118	109	103	109	112	101
Total East Europe:	107	106	110	113	113	106	106	108	107
Total East Europe and USSR:	103	107	104	116	111	101	97	107	102

Thus, objectively speaking, the Soviet bloc is facing a much bigger problem in agriculture than in any other sector of the economy. The dynamics of industrial growth have been, on the

[1] "Net agricultural production" is defined here as the value of crop production less feed, seed, and waste, plus the value of livestock production.

whole, quite satisfactory.[2] The main problem here is one of the structure of production, or how to match the actual output with effective demand. In agriculture it is essentially the problem of absolute scarcity, or how to provide enough food for the growing urban population and enough fodder for the livestock.

As the result of this dilemma, the question how to increase the agricultural output has become one of the key issues of all communist economies. Decades of willful neglect, of "hare-brained" experiments, and of deliberately starving agriculture of essential investments, have now to be paid for in terms of food shortages. Belatedly, the party leaders are now switching investment funds to the agricultural sector. But it will take years to make up for the errors of the past. Besides, many Marxist thinkers are beginning to have serious doubts as to whether the whole system of collective and state farms has an objective economic justification (151). Others openly ask whether the bloc as a whole should try to be self-sufficient in agricultural output (174). True, these are isolated voices, but the fact that such heretical views are published is a measure of the deepening crisis in East European agriculture. The very principle of state and collective ownership of land is being openly questioned. *Nova Mysl*, the theoretical organ of the Czechoslovak Party, admitted this quite openly:

> There are people who are ready with a remedy: private farming. However, under present conditions this is a trite, superficial, and in some cases demagogic suggestion. If nothing else, it does not take into account the crisis of small-scale private agricultural holdings all over the world, the very existence of which is threatened by the rapid progress of mechanization and by large-scale production technology. (40)

However, this "trite and demagogic" remedy has, in fact, already been tried by Poland and Yugoslavia where a return to private farming has brought some degree of relief from the most pressing problems of collectivized agriculture. Nevertheless, in other Soviet-bloc countries, private farming has been emphatically rejected as a viable solution of the food problem. Thus *Nova Mysl*, after deprecating the reprivatization remedy, suggested instead that the agricultural problem be attacked in the same way as the industrial

---

[2] Except for the brief stagnation period in the early sixties. See Chapter 3.

problem, i.e., through "the prudent use of material incentives by means of a system of economic levers."

We have, then, two different approaches to the agricultural dilemma in Eastern Europe. One is essentially a return to private farming, while the other calls for the application of the new model principles to the existing structure of collectivized agriculture. The qualitative difference between these two approaches makes it necessary to analyze each one separately. The Polish (and Yugoslav) way puts the main stress on increasing output (167), while in the other countries the emphasis is on maintaining so-called "socialist relations" in the countryside (119). It is the old problem of whether ideology should be given primacy over economics.

The "private ownership" solution as adopted in Poland has been a qualified success. Despite some seasonal ups and downs, unavoidable in agricultural production, the overall trend of Polish agricultural output since 1956 has been steadily upward. This has provided more ample supplies for the home market (although still inadequate by normal nutritional standards) and also a large surplus for export. Total agricultural production has risen by nearly a third, while exports have more than doubled:[3]

TABLE *3*.

Year	*Production* (1955 = 100)	*Exports*
1955	100	100
1956	107.4	85.0
1957	111.8	94.5
1958	115.1	143.4
1959	114.1	167.2
1960	129.4	177.4
1961	132.3	222.9
1962	130.1	231.1
1963	124.5	220.3
1964	126.7	221.7
1965	129.4	222.6
1966	129.1	231.7

How far this increase in production can be credited to private farming and how far to improvements in farming techniques is

[3] Table 3 is based on figures published in *Nowe Drogi*, 3 (1962) and brought up to date with figures from the Statistical Yearbook 1966 and the final economic results of 1966 published in *Trybuna Ludu* (February 8, 1967).

difficult to say. But since the performance of Polish agriculture in the recent years has been far more dynamic than that of its Czechoslovak and East German neighbors,[4] where agricultural technology is more advanced, we must assume that the incentives given to private owners have played an important part.

Until October 1956 the Polish communists pursued the orthodox agrarian policy. Peasants were forced into collective farms through a variety of pressures, and agriculture was squeezed to provide capital for industrial expansion; output stagnated. When Gomulka came to power in October 1956, he gave the peasants grudging permission to leave the collectives and return to private farming.[5] The percentage of cultivated land belonging to the socialized sector (including state farms) is today only about 14.7 per cent, while 85.3 per cent is the property of private peasants.[6]

But it was not enough to dissolve the kolkhozes. A more positive approach was needed, and this was provided by the New Agrarian Policy promulgated in January 1957 (186). Its basic features can be summarized in five points: 1) a drastic reduction in compulsory deliveries, 2) a doubling of the prices paid by the state for agricultural produce (since increased still further), 3) a reduction in taxes, 4) a guarantee of the right to private ownership of land, and 5) state help for all efficient food producers.

Needless to say, this new agrarian policy meant a complete reversal of orthodox communist practice. It not only accepted the existence of predominantly private ownership in land, but based increased food output on the principle of private profit. The individual peasants were given concrete assurances that it would pay to produce more food, not only in terms of actual cash, but, more important, in terms of supplies of scarce consumer goods and of

---

[4] Compare the relative figures in Table 2 compiled by the US Department of Agriculture.

[5] The total number of collective farms dropped from 10,510 in September 1956 to 1,803 by mid-1957. It should be noted, however, that collectivization never went very far in Poland; at its greatest extent the collectivized sector included no more than 9.2 per cent of the cultivated land (with another 13.5 per cent in state farms). Nevertheless, the collectivization drive had a catastrophic effect on private farming through its combination of discriminatory pricing, high taxes, confiscatory delivery quotas, and various "administrative" pressures.

[6] Cf. Statistical Yearbook (Warsaw 1966), p. 229.

such investment goods as building materials, tractors, agricultural machines, and fertilizers.[7]

To orthodox Marxist-Leninists this was heretical, both in theory and in practice. It meant giving priority to economic aims, i.e., agricultural production, over political aims, i.e., the socialist transformation of the countryside. It could even be called revisionism, and it was by many dogmatists in Poland as well as elsewhere in the bloc. But the policy had one essential advantage: it did produce more food.

The question naturally arises whether the party leaders regard the emphasis on private farming as a permanent policy or merely a temporary measure to give them time to overcome the problem of food shortages. No one can answer this question with any certainty. But all indications are that the present leadership in Poland has abandoned collectivization for good. For some years now responsible party leaders have not mentioned collectivization even as a distant aim. It has been quietly dropped from the party program. At the same time the party journals have been publishing articles which argue that private ownership of land is no obstacle to the socialist transformation of the countryside (167). This suggests that a substantial segment of the party establishment has reconciled itself to the abandonment of collectivization and is now seeking an ideological justification for what began as a purely pragmatic (and largely opportunistic) experiment.

Essentially two different long-term solutions are now being canvassed in Poland by various spokesmen of the party establishment. One would retain private ownership for the most part while relying for the socialist element on voluntary producers' cooperatives (collectively-owned tractors and machinery) and on the state's role as purchaser and supplier.

The other, which one may call a "biological solution," is based on the fact that the average peasant farmer is getting older because the young people are migrating to the towns. The proponents of this theory argue that existing state farms will gradually and inevitably absorb thousands of neglected or abandoned holdings,

---

[7] Most tractors and agricultural machines in Poland are collective property belonging to the peculiarly Polish institution of "agricultural circles" or quasi-voluntary producers' cooperatives.

until the bulk of the arable land in Poland passes into state ownership. But even this "biological solution" presupposes a very substantial number of privately-owned peasant holdings in the foreseeable future (152).

In coming years, then, Polish agricultural policy will operate through transactions between the state and the individual peasants. These transactions give the state a system of indirect controls over agriculture through which it can determine the structure of production and the real income of the peasants. The main lever is the price at which the peasant sells his produce.

The bulk of the agricultural output in Poland is purchased by the state under the so-called contract system (kontraktacja). The contract system gives the peasant (if he wants to use this outlet) an assured market for all the produce he may want to sell. Since the contracts are signed for future deliveries (i.e., for next years's grain or meat), the peasant can calculate his income well in advance. Many contracts provide fringe benefits (such as stated quantities of coal at reduced prices). This system has definite advantages from the point of view of the peasant, since it eliminates many of the risks inherent in agricultural production (148).

The contract system permits the state to influence directly the structure of future agricultural output. By offering better prices and additional fringe benefits for a particular product, the state can induce the peasants to grow more grain rather than potatoes or vice versa. If more beef is required rather than pork, a higher contract price for one and a lower for the other usually bring the desired changes in the pattern of animal breeding. The contract system is thus a valuable instrument of planning.

The contract system is also a good example of indirect controls applied predominantly through the market mechanism. But it creates only an imperfect market, since there is no interplay of supply and demand in the accepted sense, no room for bargaining between seller and purchaser. The contracts are offered by the state on a take-it-or-leave-it basis, with prices and fringe benefits predetermined. Thus the contract system is predominantly an instrument of policy and planning and lacks the flexibility of a true market mechanism.

However, no peasant is forced to use the contract system. He is free to sell all his marketable surplus after he has delivered his compulsory quotas, on the so-called "free market."[8] Here the peasant deals essentially with two categories of buyers: the state procurement office and individual customers. In theory this is a genuine free market with prices determined by the interplay of supply and demand. In reality, only a fraction of the marketable surplus is sold under genuinely free market conditions. For the rest there is again only one monopolistic buyer—the state.

The limitations of the "free market" stem partly from circumstances. Basic produce such as grain and meat and even fruits and vegetables can as a rule be sold only to the state. Except for a few private millers, butchers, and grocers, there is no other outlet for these things. The state not only has a monopoly of bulk buying (there being no private wholesalers in Poland) but remains the peasant's only customer outside of the licensed market places.

But the limitations of the free market also result from a deliberate policy of reducing the peasant's bargaining power. While the authorities make every effort to promote producers' cooperatives in the countryside, they do not allow the peasants to organize sellers' cooperatives. Nor are the state-run restaurants, hotels, butcher shops, etc., allowed to buy their supplies directly from the producers; the communists who denounce so loudly the wickedness of middlemen in the West have made their own domain into a middleman's paradise.

With all their imperfections, however, the Polish reforms did reintroduce elements of a market mechanism in agriculture. They also replaced direct controls by indirect ones, helping to restore the balance between peasant incomes and the earnings of industrial workers. Indeed, the real incomes of peasants in Poland have been

---

[8] The compulsory quotas are the vestiges of the old compulsory delivery system that was the predominant form of marketing before the agricultural reforms of 1957. They are no longer very significant, since the total volume of produce delivered in this way amounts to only about 7 per cent of the marketable output. They are really a form of tax, and the state's proceeds from them (i.e., the difference between the prices fixed for compulsory delivery quotas and the "normal" contract or free market prices) are mainly used to finance the purchase of tractors and machinery for the agricultural circles. Each community is credited with the difference between the contract value of its aggregate deliveries and the compulsory delivery price. The bulk of this fund is put at the disposal of the local agricultural circle and may be used for the purchase of machinery or for approved forms of investment.

growing at a faster rate than the average real wage. During 1961–65, for instance, the net real incomes of the peasants (i.e., after deducting investment expenditure) increased by 12 per cent while the average real wage rose by only 8 per cent.[9] Again in 1966 the real wage of the workers had increased by 3 per cent, while the net real incomes of the peasants had increased by 5 per cent (184).

Let us now examine the other approach to agricultural reform, that which rejects private ownership of land and seeks instead to apply the principles of the new economic model in industry to the existing structure of agriculture. This does not mean that this more "socialist" alternative (to use the expression of *Nova Mysl* as quoted at the beginning of this chapter) makes no use of private initiative; on the contrary it relies heavily on the output of household plots. These used to be regarded as "survivals of the past," and for a while efforts were made to restrict them, but pragmatic common sense has now prevailed and the usefulness of private plots is again being stressed by party spokesmen.

Hungary has gone furthest in this. There we see something like the ideological rehabilitation of household plots. Hungarian leaders emphasize again and again that "private plots are not a temporary solution but an organic and permanent feature of collective farming" (121). The chief aim of this propaganda is to convince the Hungarian collective farmers that their family plots will never be taken away.

The productivity of the household plot is now admitted, in fact heavily stressed. As Central Committee secretary Karoly Nemeth said, "private plots are an important and valuable part of our national wealth and their productive possibilities should be utilized to the utmost." These plots, he added, comprise only 9.6 per cent of the arable land, but supply about half the people with their milk and dairy products, poultry and eggs, and 30 per cent with their fruit and vegetables.[10] The peasants are now given strong incentives to produce as much food as possible on their

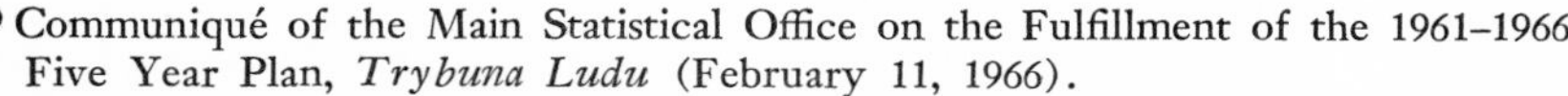

[9] Communiqué of the Main Statistical Office on the Fulfillment of the 1961–1966 Five Year Plan, *Trybuna Ludu* (February 11, 1966).

[10] The Nemeth speech was reported in *Nepszabadsag* (December 3, 1963). According to other sources, private plots supply 11 per cent of the pigs, 84 per cent of piglets, 30.9 per cent of milk, 15.5 per cent of poultry, 50.9 per cent of eggs. Cf. P. Alle, "The Role of Private Plots" (95).

small piece of land. Liberal credits are granted for purchase of livestock. Common pastures are opened to privately-owned animals. The state even provides dry fodder for private livestock at nominal cost.

The need to ensure food supplies is likewise the motive for the Bulgarian leadership's support of household plots. While the Hungarians are ahead in theory, having rehabilitated household plots ideologically, the Bulgarians have gone much further in the practical application of material incentives. A decree issued in Sofia early in February 1963 made the ownership of private plots permanent and hereditary. It also stipulated that the produce grown on those plots should be free from taxation and not subject to state procurement, unless voluntarily contracted for. The livestock raised on private plots might be grazed on state-owned meadows free of charge (15).

The Bulgarians have even gone so far as to create new private holdings. The same decree provided for the distribution of all uncultivated and abandoned land to practically anybody who wanted to apply for it, and the ownership was to be hereditary.

The preamble to the Bulgarian decree informs the local party and government officials that it is their duty to help every citizen produce as much food as possible on his private plot. The decree warns that "the performance of local party secretaries, government officials and collective farm chairmen will be judged not only by the output of state farms and collective farms, but also by the quantity of produce grown on the private plots."

The economic importance of household plots (especially in livestock production) is shown by the following figures taken from official sources, which give the percentage share of private plots in total production (254):

TABLE 4.

	Meat	*Milk*	*Eggs*
USSR	46	45	78
Hungary	64	60	90
Czechoslovakia	25	28	56
Bulgaria	27	26	50
Rumania	about 40 per cent of output		

A real solution to the farm problem, however, will require a significant increase in the productivity of the socialized sector which comprises most of the cultivated land. Some of the bloc countries (including the Soviet Union itself) are emphasizing a quantitative increase (rather substantial to be sure) in investment outlays and supplies of artificial fertilizers, as well as in prices paid for agricultural produce. Others (for instance Czechoslovakia and Hungary) want to apply the principles of the new economic model to agriculture.

An example of the conservative, i.e., quantitative approach is an article in the authoritative *Selskaya Zhizn* (September 22, 1966) attacking Soviet economists who have suggested that the law of supply and demand should play a bigger role in agricultural policy. The article rejected the thesis that direct and detailed planning of crops and delivery quotas is inefficient. "The implementation of those (supply and demand) suggestions" could "hamper the further growth of agriculture and the entire national economy." The Soviet daily asserted that "centralized planning of the procurement of agricultural produce is imperative," and that "the government is unable to relinquish control of the supply of food for the population and raw materials for industry." It said that the present system of fixed prices "protects our kolkhozes and sovkhozes from the hazards of market competition and assures their financial stability. They need a guaranteed demand for their products at guaranteed prices" (214).

A markedly different attitude prevails in Czechoslovakia and Hungary. *Rude Pravo* confirmed on August 24, 1966 that the principles of the new economic model would be "comprehensively" applied to Czechoslovak agriculture on January 1, 1967. It explained that new prices were to be established based on production costs and on supply and demand (67). This was merely an elaboration of the March 1966 decision taken by the party Central Committee, which contained the blueprint for the reform of agricultural management (77). The existing organizational structure of Czechoslovak agriculture is to remain intact, but the principle of directive control is to be replaced by a new one: that of maximizing the gross income of collective farms (JZD) and state farms. This maximizing of income is intended as an incentive to increased investment, and not to raising the earnings of the farmers. While the state farm managers and the JZD chairmen are to have greater latitude in planning their output structure and more say in how it is sold, the official intent is that wages of agricultural workers are to remain stable, at least for the first few years of the new system (82). Moreover, the tax structure is to be adjusted to induce a flow of funds away from individual remuneration and into capital accumulation.

One interesting feature of the new model for Czechoslovak agriculture is that the laws and regulations pertaining to household plots and the marginal residue of private peasant farming are to remain unchanged. Apparently the Czechoslovak leadership, unlike the Hungarian and the Bulgarian, wishes to keep private initiative in agriculture to a minimum. The ideological explanation for this was provided by Central Committee secretary Lubomir Strougal, who declared in effect that the decision to collectivize agricultural was a political one and the "socialist transformation of the countryside" could not be modified to fit merely economic considerations (55). Thus the Czechoslovaks want only to make the existing system more efficient and more responsive to needs. But even this will require them to introduce "certain elements of a market mechanism and some decentralization of economic decision making" (22).

The principle of fixed prices is to be retained for all staple agricultural produce. However, the element of cost will play a great part in determining the uniform procurement prices. In addition, to "ensure a flexible reaction to the quick changes in the supply and demand position," the Czechoslovak blueprint foresees that "centrally defined premiums" may be added to the uniform purchasing prices (77). On top of that the price may be hiked still higher by "supplements" paid for produce in especially short supply. There will also be "variable prices" and "free prices" for a limited category of produce.

The Czechoslovak blueprint states that "collective farms (JZD) and state farms, as independent production and economic entities, are the basic and predominant production units in agriculture." But this "independence" is substantially limited by centralized planning. In principle, the individual farms can make their own annual plans on the basis of their contractual arrangement with state procurement centers. They also exercise "concrete choice" with regard to the structure of their output (82). But the Ministry of Agriculture retains a commanding position in the final acceptance and harmonization of individual plans. By comparison, the margin of decision granted to Hungarian collectives and state farms seems to be much greater. They are to be allowed to grow what they judge to be most profitable, with the exception of grain quotas imposed from above (109).

The main instrument of market relations in Czechoslovak agriculture is to be the contract signed annually by the farm and the state procurement center. Their relations are supposed to be based on "the principle of equality of supplier and consumer" (77). But, as we have seen in the case of Poland, the very fact that the "consumer" enjoys a total monopoly of purchases makes the market very imperfect.

The detailed pattern of the Hungarian economic reforms is not yet as clear as in Czechoslovakia. One thing is certain, however: Budapest intends to place much more stress on the output of private farming. Perhaps this is because of the greater economic importance of the private sector in Hungarian agriculture. Some 16.1 per cent of the arable land (including private plots), as well as 55.2 per cent of the orchards and vegetable gardens and 64.9 per cent of the vineyards are still privately owned.[11] But as in Czechoslovakia, real progress will have to come from higher productivity in the collective and state farms. There are at present 3,400 collectives in Hungary cultivating 81.7 per cent of the agricultural land[12] and it is on them that the battle for more food will be decided.

The Hungarian agricultural reforms are based on three elements: more autonomy for the collectives, which are to be treated as independent enterprises; higher procurement prices; and new methods of state purchasing.

As far as the autonomy of the collective farms is concerned, the extent of it was described at length in an article written by the Deputy Minister of Agriculture Janos Keseru and published by the official party daily *Nepszabadsag* (109). Here are the most relevant excerpts of this article, which spotlight the nature of the changes and the rationale behind them as seen by the Kadar regime:

> One of the prominent features of the economic reform is the change of the relationships between the enterprises and the managing bodies.

---

[11] *Statisztikai Evkonyv* (Statistical Yearbook) 1965.

[12] Ibid., also *Statisztikai Szemle*, 2 (1966).

The change serves to develop a greater independence of the enterprises, while, at the same time, a suitable number of means are concentrated in the hands of central management, which will ensure the efficient carrying through of economic-political aims and decisions, and also the order desired in economic life outside the enterprises, without jeopardizing the assertion of greater independence of individual agricultural enterprises.

One of the most important new features is that those economic decisions, for which the local knowledge of enterprise leaders and workers is indispensable, will be handed down by the managing bodies to the enterprise. In the agricultural collectives, for example, the economic decisions connected with the production profile of the individual cooperatives will be taken away from the managing bodies and handed over to the level of cooperative leadership. It is obvious that in agriculture—in which local conditions, natural resources and other factors are in such close relation to the actual production—collective leaders and members can decide best, because they know local conditions better than anyone else. . . .

In general, the agricultural collectives have to decide how to utilize their produce and whom they will sell it to. And also in what form it will be sold: whether raw, semi-finished or ready for consumption. The right of decision in these questions belongs to the cooperative, which is a collective enterprise under the ownership of the members. These members have to live on the income collected from the sale of the produce. A practice which would force on them disadvantageous forms of selling, would also infringe upon their rights and at the same time impair their financial income. . . .

Most of the investments are now to be made from the cooperatives' own resources [credits] and therefore these have a direct impact on the financial situation of the membership. This is why it was necessary to remove the right to decide on investments from the central managing bodies and transfer it to the level of the agricultural collectives. They have to decide, to specify the circumstances, the method of their implementation, etc. Only those large investments are an exception to the rule which concern several enterprises, and most of which are implemented through state subsidy—but of these there are relatively few in agriculture.

Decisions in connection with the use of the financial fund which the collectives have at their disposal and the net income will also be handled by the leadership of the farmers' collective. In this field, too, central management has to limit its interference and impose fewer commitments. Except for complying with a few stipulations protecting over-all social interest, the agricultural collectives have the right of free decision in matters such as the extent of reserves, their utilization and purpose, the use of the income, etc.

We have thus ample proof that in the new economic mechanism not only will the number of decisions at an enterprise level grow, but that "far-reaching" decisions, too, which will basically influence the life and activities in the enterprise, will likewise increase. Hence, enterprise decisions will also undergo a change from the viewpoint of quality. (109)

In short, the principle of extensive autonomy for the collectives is based on the aim of "reducing administrative interference . . . and using material incentives to induce the collectives to produce what is most advantageous, both to them and to the whole economy" (111). With the exception of grain crops (for which the growing area used in 1964 must remain unchanged) the collectives will be free to determine for themselves how they want to shape their production plans and what they want to grow. The only way in which the central planners may influence those decisions is by the use of economic levers, i.e., by raising and lowering procurement prices (100). This is indeed an important step toward introducing market conditions in agriculture.

To ensure the profitable operation of autonomous collectives, the Hungarians will raise procurement prices (107). How this price mechanism will operate is not yet clear, since the Hungarian regime apparently wants to use both prices and subsidies so as to level out the advantages of collective farms operating on better soil. It is quite conceivable that variable tax rates will also be applied to compensate for natural disadvantages. This is again a step in the right direction since it introduces the necessary degree of flexibility into a hitherto rigid and uniform policy. However, as in Czechoslovakia most agricultural procurement prices are still to be fixed by the state, with only a marginal amount of output being sold at "variable" and free prices (100).

Important inroads will be made also into the state's monopoly of purchasing. Certain staple produce (such as grain) will still be sold only to state procurement agencies, but other products can be sold directly to processing plants, hotels, restaurants, or consumers (107). Collectives will be permitted to conclude long-term delivery contracts with permanent users of their products. Collective farms will also be allowed to process their own goods when this is more economical (111). And the bargaining position of the collectives vis-à-vis the state is to be substantially strengthened. Each collective will have the right to choose the procurement agency with which it prefers to deal. Thus some degree of competition is to be introduced into a field where until now completely monopolistic conditions and administrative pressures have prevailed.

Last, but not least, the Kadar regime has now promised to the collective farmers that it will regulate the thorny problem of the ownership of land cultivated by Hungarian cooperatives. At present 78 per cent of this land is still (at least nominally) the private property of the members; while the remaining 22 per cent is owned by the state (119). The proposed new measures have both ideological implications and a very practical meaning. The intention is to raise the concept of "collective ownership" to the equal status (ideologically) with "state ownership." This would create a basis for making all land actually used by the cooperatives their "collectively owned property." Nominally, this land is now only "leased," both from the state and from the private owners (collective farm members). Obviously the Hungarian regime hopes that by transferring this land to "collective ownership" it would strengthen the existing cooperatives and give them the necessary vested interest in becoming a fully fledged agricultural enterprise. Incidentally, "a suitable compensation" is to be paid by the collective farms for the land so acquired both to the state and to the private owners, who are expected to offer their land to the collective on a "voluntary basis."

Whether the Hungarian collectives will take advantage of this opportunity to acquire the ownership title to the land they now formally lease, is by no means certain. The financial expenditure involved is bound to go beyond the means of the average collective farm. So the new form of "collective property" has to be regarded rather as a long-term objective, for which no practical provisions have yet been made.

In a sense the same could be said about all other reform proposals pertaining to Hungarian agriculture. What has been published so far amounts to a set of rather vague principles, which have yet to be translated into definite measures. But even those general principles seem to justify the regime's claim that for the Hungarian agriculture "one epoch has come to an end and a new epoch has begun" (104).

EPILOGUE

The inevitable time gap arising from printing schedules makes it necessary to update somewhat my progress report on economic reforms in Eastern Europe. While the analytical portions of this book stood up well to the passage of time, the descriptive chapters have to be supplemented by at least a brief outline of the developments in the second half of 1967 and early 1968. Generally speaking, the momentum of the reform movement throughout Eastern Europe has been maintained although there were no really new elements in the over-all situation, except, perhaps, for the introduction of the mini-reform in Rumania. But within this general trend there emerged—perhaps more clearly than before—two distinct groups of countries: the pace-setters and the feet-draggers.

While Yugoslavia continued to lead the field and, in terms of abandoning the rules of a command economy, even increased the distance dividing it from the Moscow bloc members, the rest of the countries subject to this survey became more firmly divided into the protagonists of integral, all-embracing economic reforms and the adherents of patchwork, step by step methods. Thus Czechoslovakia and (as of January 1, 1968) Hungary have now changed over completely to the new economic model, while the Soviet Union, Poland, and Bulgaria were apparently quite satisfied with introducing some degree of economic rationalism into the old arbitrary system. With the passage of time, it now seems more and more obvious that the difference between the two types of reform concepts is quantitative rather than qualitative. The East German pragmatic and yet arbitrary model still stands apart from either the pace-setters and the feet-draggers, since—while rational and pragmatic—it contains strong elements of the specific teutonic authoritarian and arbitrary paternalism. The embryo-reforms in Rumania must, at least for the time being, be classified as nothing else but pragmatic improvements, superimposed on a system which still remains essentially a centralistic command economy.

The real purpose of this epilogue is not so much to bring all the factual parts of this book up to date, which would be a well-nigh impossible task, but to give the reader a bird's-eye view of the most pertinent developments as far as the economic reform movement in Eastern Europe is concerned, in the time lag between the writing of the manuscript and the printing. With this purpose in mind I would now review the situation on those sectors where such descriptive updating seems indispensable.

I have repeatedly stressed in this book that economic reforms—however comprehensively and conscientiously applied—cannot be regarded as a sort of panacea for all the economic ills of a typical communist planned economy. I have also warned again and again that the economic situation of individual countries may well get worse before it gets better. The first year of Czechoslovakia's practical experiences with the new economic model has fully confirmed those analytical assumptions. Economic reforms in Czechoslovakia have run into serious trouble because chronic and acute economic problems, inherited from the past era, prevented their full realization. Those difficulties have been magnified by the fact that—at least until the dramatic ouster of Novotny (early January 1968)—the leadership of the communist party of Czechoslovakia has been implementing the new pragmatic measures in a half-hearted way, reducing them more often than not to an empty shell.

As the result, the first year of the new economic model was anything but a success. Because of undue interference of the bureaucratic infrastructure, the reform of wholesale prices resulted in a huge amount of unearned income accruing to the mammoth supply enterprises. According to official estimates, by the end of 1967 wholesale prices in Czechoslovakia were expected to rise by 19 per cent over their average level on January 1, 1966. In fact they increased by some 30 per cent. Although this raise of wholesale prices was not yet reflected in the cost of living (retail prices have increased in 1967 by only 1.1 per cent), it had—nevertheless—

serious economic repercussions. Apart from the huge unearned income of monopolistic supply enterprises (estimated at sixteen billion crowns), this rapid growth of wholesale prices defeated one of the main purposes of the new measures, namely the elimination of inefficient and marginal producers. Under the prevailing prices level every enterprise was able to show a profit, regardless of its efficiency standards.

With such a large amount of disposable income, the Czechoslovak enterprises were able to hire more workers and pay them higher wages. This resulted in a substantial increase in personal incomes (3.6 per cent, as against the anticipated 2 per cent). At the same time the shortages on the market persisted, with no prospects for a change for the better. As one Slovak economist put it "the enterprises have so much money that they are not really interested in adapting their output to the needs of the market, they prefer to take advantage of their monopolistic position to dictate their own prices. . . . The monopoly enjoyed by many producers enables them to look down on the buyers and dictate their own conditions."[1]

The huge increases in the enterprise incomes and the steady growth of personal earnings, coupled with a persistent shortage of consumer goods and industrial supplies, inevitably intensified the latent inflationary pressures within Czechoslovak economy. Such pressures could only be held in check—and very imperfectly at that—by reimposing stricter control of both retail and supply prices, i.e., by perpetuating the worst features of the old arbitrary system. Indeed, *Rude Pravo* warned solemnly in October 1967 that "inflationary tendencies are endangering the future of the new system of management itself. Unless the enterprises show sufficient understanding of the present economic situation and economic policy, tendencies may well grow supporting the return to the old administrative system."[2]

Despite such self-righteous statements, the policy inertia of the Czechoslovak ruling oligarchy did carry a large share of the blame

---

[1] Dr. E. Mikula, "Never Mind the Old School Tie—Leave Those Pear Trees Alone," *Lud* [Bratislava] (September 3, 1967).

[2] Z. Sulc, "The Responsibility of the Enterprise and of the Center," *Rude Pravo* (October 3, 1967).

for the growth of those inflationary pressures, to which it, perhaps, contributed as much as the selfish behavior of monopolistic enterprises. First of all, the Czech authorities ignored persistent warnings of the people who have worked out the principles of the new model (such as Professor O. Sik) that the monopolistic structure of Czechoslovak industry and the resulting lack of market competition would tend to frustrate the consumer-oriented measures introduced in 1967. They also resisted persistent demands that "market shortages should be alleviated by imports."[3] However, it was in the sector of foreign trade policy (still under full state control) that the central authorities did the most damage, in terms of contributing to the growth of inflationary pressures.

The problem is that purely political considerations (despite the verbal declarations of the regime's spokesmen to the contrary) still determined (at least until the fall of Novotny) the basic priorities of Czechoslovak foreign trade. And while there is some truth in the official claims that objective difficulties (in terms of low quality and outdated technology) frustrated the much-heralded export offensive in the industrialized West, the main reason for the persistent deficit trade balances with the hard currency countries were politically motivated priorities granted to exports to the third world (especially Middle East) and the Comecon area. The fact is that Czechoslovak foreign trade has been deliberately excluded from the modus operandi of the new economic model and subordinated to purely political considerations.

As the result, all throughout 1967 Czechoslovakia has been adding up to its already considerable surplus trade balance with the Comecon countries, while at the same time pouring unrequited exports to Middle East and other third world areas. Such trade policy contributed considerably to the growth of inflationary pressures, by draining the home market of scarce supplies. At the same time, the potential hard currency earnings were being deliberately forsaken, thus limiting the room for maneuver available to central authorities in respect of promoting a certain degree of competition by consumer goods imports.

But whatever the defects of their economic policies, the main

---

[3] J. Kosta and A. Cervenkova, "It Is Not a Question of the Economic Balance Alone," *Literarni Noviny* (May 27, 1967).

charge against Novotny and his associates has been that they lacke[d] the political will to carry out the new model measures to their logical conclusion, in obvious deference to the vested interests of the bureaucratic infrastructure. As the result of this ambivalent attitude the protagonists of the new economic model joined forces with the political opponents of Novotny and brought about his downfall. Political logic would indicate that the Dubcek group, which has ruled Czechoslovakia since January 1968, would now pay greater attenion to the demands of economic reformers, if only to pay for their political support during the recent power struggle. But then the rules of political logic are not always valid in the specific conditions of a communist mono-party system.

I have dwelt a little longer on Czechoslovak events, since this is the only country (except for Yugoslavia, of course) which, at the time of writing, has had any sort of macro-economic experiences with the integral application of the modus operandi of the new economic model. Since January 1, 1968, Hungary is also in the running. But, perhaps with a weary eye on the problems which the Czech communists had to face, the Hungarian oligarchy took infinite pains to avoid the costly mistakes of their northern neighbors.

Hungarian economic reform is not only more comprehensive, but was definitely better prepared, at least in the administrative and legal sense, than the Czechoslovak. All throughout 1967 the government in Budapest had been issuing literally dozens of decrees, creating the legal and administrative framework for a smooth operation of the new economic model. This legislative process, although in itself arbitrary and autocratic, has decisively weakened the grip of the bureaucratic infrastructure over the Hungarian economy. So much so, that the Hungarian Minister of Justice was able to state at a press conference that "in the future the economic activity of state enterprises will not be, in any way, regulated by central institutions. The law merely stipulates that, in its economic activity, each enterprise ought to make the most sensible use of its productive potential."[4]

The law in question, the Hungarian decree on state enterprises,

---

[4] Interview with Minister of Justice, Mihaly Korom, *Nepszabadsag* (May 13, 1967).

kind in the Moscow bloc, has filled one of the most reform blueprints, a gap which I have fre- out in my book. It is a legal measure, which is a Charta of a truly independent socialized enter- e same time it is thoroughly permeated by the consumer-oriented and efficiency-conscious eco- model. The very first article of this decree states that "the main task of the state enterprise is to contribute by its efficient activity to the satisfaction of the needs of the society."[5]

The decree also stipulates that it is the duty of the central institutions to set up state enterprises, to provide them with the initial capital and operational funds, and then not to interfere into their normal economic operations. After dispensing their tax obligations toward the state, the enterprises retain all the profits they earned. The sphere of responsibility of the enterprise director has been greatly enlarged and clearly defined. He sets up the production plans, he establishes the rules concerning the conditions of work and pay, as well as the internal organization, he negotiates with trade unions about wage rates, and he makes all the decisions concerning credits, investments (financed out of the enterprise's own resources), questions of merger with other enterprises, etc.[6] Thus, the prerogatives of the enterprise director in Hungary are infinitely greater than elsewhere in the bloc.

Among the multitude of other decrees, the one concerning a new system of profit-sharing also deserves mention. Apart from detailed provisions how the profits of socialized enterprises ought to be divided, so that their proper long term functioning would be ensured (the problems of capital amortization investment fund and adequate profit and loss reserves), the decree also regulates the question of material incentives arising from the profit-sharing principle. It stipulates precisely what portion of the net profit should be made available for distribution and in what way it ought to be distributed.

In this respect all personnel of a state enterprise are classified into three categories. The manager and his immediate assistants

[5] Decree No. 11 of the Hungarian Revolutionary Workers and Peasants Government, *Magyar Kozlony* [Budapest] (May 13, 1967).

[6] Ibid.

belong to the first category; the supervisory personnel, down to the foreman level and the top administrative employees belong to the second one; and the rest are all classified in the third category. This subdivision is not only pertinent in respect to participation in profits and thus in the sense of rewarding a greater degree of responsibility, but also indicates the difference in bearing the entrepreneurial risks.

As far as profit-sharing is concerned, the Hungarian decree stipulates that the top managerial group can be rewarded from this source up to the amount equivalent to 80 per cent of their yearly salaries. In contrast the profit shares of the people in category 2 cannot exceed 50 per cent of their yearly earnings and for category 3 this figure drops to 15 per cent. However, the workers and lower grade office employees, who belong to this lowest category, enjoy full state guarantee for their earnings. Whether the enterprise operates at a profit or shows a loss, they are entitled to receive their wages in full and for this purpose they have the first claim on all enterprise's assets. In contrast, the state guarantee covers only 75 per cent of the yearly salaries of the top managerial group. The remaining 25 per cent are paid out to them only if the enterprise concerned shows a profit at the end of the financial year. The same principle applies to the supervisory staff, only the corresponding figures are: 85 per cent of the yearly salary guaranteed, 15 per cent depending on the results of the profit and loss account.[7] Thus, the decree provides a clear link between income differentiation on one side and entrepreneurial functions and risk bearing on the other.

Finally, a few words have to be said about the Hungarian price reform, which came into effect on January 1, 1968. Unlike similar reforms elsewhere, the Hungarian affects both wholesale and retail prices and has been introduced at one throw. The general principles of the Hungarian reform are almost the same, as in the case of Czechoslovakia and those have been amply discussed in Chapter 4. The only difference is that while in Czechoslovakia there are three categories of prices (fixed, fluctuating between the upper and the lower limit, and free), the Hungarians have added

---

[7] Decree No. 19 issued by the Economic Committee of the Hungarian Council of Ministers, *Muszaki Elet* (June 15, 1967).

a fourth category—"prices fixed according to regulations issued by central authorities."

We are still lacking the official elaboration as to what those regulations may pertain to. What is known is that all prices in this category are to be determined at the factory level (in the same way as the free prices), but that certain regulations issued by central authorities must be adhered to. Presumably those regulations will not affect price determination process as such, but rather quality and design of the product.

Hungarian authorities are predicting that, as the result of their comprehensive price reform, the general level of retail prices will increase no more than 2 to 3 per cent by the end of 1968. Thus, no significant growth of inflationary pressures is expected. But the Kadar regime is taking no chances. To counteract the expected 4 to 6 per cent increase in the free and fluctuating prices categories (comprising 70 to 75 per cent of all consumer goods), huge price reductions were introduced at the beginning of 1968, including radio and TV sets and some articles of clothing. Also, bearing in mind the Czechoslovak experience, the Hungarian authorities have armed themselves with special measures to prevent "illegal profiteering." All profits, resulting from "unjustified price increases" or exceeding "reasonable profit rate" (except where earned through "higher efficiency") will be subject to additional tax assessment. Whether those vaguely worded regulations would prevent an inflationary price spiral is, perhaps, questionable. One may rather fear that they would provide the thin edge of the wedge, as far as bureaucratic interference is concerned.

As already indicated, Czechoslovakia and Hungary were the pace-setters of the reform movement in Eastern Europe. In contrast, the Soviet Union, Bulgaria, and Poland have barely maintained the momentum of their respective reforms. The changes, if they occurred at all, were quantitative rather than qualitative. Nevertheless, some progress has to be registered. The Soviet Union, for instance, began to implement the reform of wholesale prices on the lines indicated in Chapter 4. Also the number of enterprises working according to the system has grown considerably. According to official estimates, at the beginning of 1968 some 5,500 Soviet enterprises accounting for about one-third of the global industrial output were operating in accordance with the new rules of management and planning.[8] Otherwise, however, there were no new developments on the sector of economic reforms.

In Bulgaria the second of the several phases of the economic reform is to be implemented in 1968. A special decree "on Increasing the Profitability of the Economy" has been published late in 1967,[9] ostensibly to speed up some of the pragmatic measures envisaged in the "Theses" of December 1965. The decree, which reiterates most of the provisions contained in original "Theses," contains also in its preamble a frank admission that very little has been done so far. The future is also rather uncertain. Although the October 1967 decree sets firm deadlines for putting into effect certain pragmatic measures, such as greater managerial prerogatives; investments from enterprise-owned resources, or financed by a bank loan, instead of state budget; greater incentives for market-oriented production, etc.—the actual reforms it envisages are hedged with many safeguards, all aiming at maintaining centralistic control. Moreover, the decree's proposed remedy for raising labor productivity is the arch-stalinist medicine of an increase in work norms. On the whole, the October 1967 decree is a mixed bag. It contains some provisions which may well tend to promote profit-consciousness of individual enterprises, but it also exemplifies the typical Bulgarian fear of dispensing with bureaucratic control and purely dogmatic short-term solutions.

The same kind of top level inertia prevails in Poland, where even potentially positive measures are being applied in a patchwork manner and then neutralized by a growing tendency for infrastructural interference. True, the dangerously precarious state of Polish economy makes the introduction of pragmatic reforms more risky than elsewhere, but even so the almost complete lack of progress is rather disappointing. In the country which had pioneered economic reforms more than eleven years ago, most of the practical implementation is still at the stage of isolated experiments. There are also endless discussions how to adjust the generally accepted reform concepts to Polish economy reality. But as a regime's own periodical pointed out, "the main problem lies not

---

[8] *Trud* (January 9, 1968).

[9] Decree No. 88 of the Central Committee and the Bulgarian Council of Ministers of 14 October 1967, *Darzhaven Vestnik* (November 10, 1967).

so much in the necessity of adjusting the concepts, as in the insistence of consistent implementation in practice of the accepted principles. . . ."[10]

In Rumania, after several months of soul-searching, the regime came out with its own mini-reform. In October 1967 the Central Committee approved draft directives for perfecting management and planning of the national economy. Those draft directives were unanimously approved by a specially convened National Party Conference in December 1967. All in all, the blueprint for this mini-reform is a curious document, a typically Rumanian mixture of dynamic conservatism, combined with an ardent desire to acquire up-to-date techniques of a modern industrial state. But in this case the Rumanian passion for "uniqueness" may well prove the undoing of the regime's new economic program. For while sensible steps are outlined in the directives for improving the present Rumanian economic system, the mini-reform blueprint neither presents a consistent picture of a viable economic model, nor does it provide for sufficient changes to allow the Rumanian economy to adapt itself to the requirements of the modern industrial society.

Thus the Rumanian directives increase the area of responsibility of the enterprise-level management, without however providing those managers with sufficient prerogatives. Nor does it indicate sufficient institutional changes to undo the centralistic organizational structure of Rumanian economy. Quite the contrary. If anything has been strengthened, it is the bureaucratic superstructure and its powers of control.

Thus, in their pursuit of the "Rumanian way," in the field of economic reforms, Ceausescu and his associates are attempting to prove that an industrially developing economy can maintain rigid central planning, based on detailed compulsory indicators, and still achieve significant improvements through limited steps to rationalize and decentralize selected areas of economic activity. There is no evidence in the experiences of other countries, which have passed through Rumania's present stage of industrialization, that such an approach will solve any of the basic problems.

So much for a bird's-eye view of country by country develop-

---

[10] J. G., "The Reform and Men," *Zycie Gospodarcze* (July 30, 1967).

ments. A few words should also be said about the continuing search of trade unions, particularly the Hungarian ones, for their proper role in the new economic model. Such search is still going on. The controversial right of veto has not been clearly defined, either at the Hungarian Trade Union Congress (May 1967), nor in the more recently enacted New Labor Code. This much heralded legal document proved to be nothing more than a set of basic rules, which left the detailed regulation of the labor-management relations to be determined by collective contracts negotiated at the enterprise level.

Although the fact that essential problems concerning conditions of work and pay are now subject to negotiations between the unions and the enterprise management must be considered a major step forward, no final judgment can be passed on the new role of the Hungarian unions until the actual contents of some representative collective labor contracts have been studied in detail.

To sum up, in the second half of 1967 and the early months of 1968, some progress has to be acknowledged. But the pace—except in a few selected sectors—remains painfully slow.

BIBLIOGRAPHY OF WORKS CITED

BULGARIA

Articles and periodicals

1 Kunin, P. "The Systematic Development of the National Economy, According to the Plan and to the Principle from Each According to His Ability, to Each According to His Work, under Socialism," *Novo Vreme* [Sofia], 12 (December 1963).

2 Lyutov, A. "New Way of Planning, or Rejection of Planning," *Rabotnichesko Delo* [Sofia] (January 16, 1966).

3 Miloshevsky, A. "On the Question of Strengthening Economic Incentives in our Country," *Novo Vreme*, 11 (November 1963).

4 Miranov, J. "Problems of Internal Economic Accounting when Wage Payments Are Linked to Enterprise Financial and Economic Results," *Finansi i Kredit* [Sofia], 7 (July 1964).

5 Mishev, M. "Rational Use of Labor Resources," *Rabotnichesko Delo* (January 28, 1967).

6 Petrov, G. "New Way of Planning," *Rabotnichesko Delo* (January 13, 1967).

7 ———. "To Raise the Efficiency of the Management of the Economy," a series of articles in the provincial paper *Radopsky Ustrem* (September 22, 24, 26, and 29, 1964).

8 Savov, M. and N. Velichkov. "The Problems of Adjusting Domestic Prices to International Prices," *Ikonomicheska Misal* [Sofia], 9 (September 1966).

9 Unsigned. "Under New Conditions," *Partyien Zhivot* [Sofia], 13 (September 1965), 3–9.

10 Unsigned. "For a Nation-Wide Discussion," *Rabotnichesko Delo* (September 5, 1965).

Official Documents and Statements

11 "The Politburo Theses on the New System of Planning and Management of National Economy," *Rabotnichesko Delo* (December 4, 1965).

12 First Secretary T. Zhivkov's Report at the April 1966 Central Committee Plenum, *Rabotnichesko Delo* (April 29, 1966).

13 Resolution of April 1966 Central Committee Plenum *Rabotnichesko Delo* (April 29, 1966).

14 The Decree of the Bulgarian Council of Ministers, "On Solving Some Problems Connected with the Efficient Use of Labor Resources," *Darzhaven Vestnik* [Sofia] (January 27, 1967).

15 The Decree of the Bulgarian Central Committee and the Council of Ministers, "Development of Livestock Breeding on Private Plots of Collective Farmers and Cultivation of all Waste and Abandoned Land on the Outskirts of Towns and Villages," *Rabotnichesko Delo* (February 3, 1963).

Secondary Sources

16 Brown, J. F. "Reforms in Bulgaria," *Problems of Communism* (May–June 1966).

17 Lendvai, P. "Bulgaria Steers a New Course," *East Europe* (October 1965).

CZECHOSLOVAKIA

Articles and periodicals

18 Bistrina, I. "New System and Democracy," *Literarni Noviny* [Prague] (December 7, 1966).

19 Cipek, K. "The Economists of the European Socialist Countries on Models of Management of the Economy and of Enterprises," *Politicka Ekonomie* [Prague], 5 (May 1966).

20 Fojtik, J. "Does a Socialist Man Exist," *Rude Pravo* [Prague] (January 5, 1967).

21 Havel, V. and L. Petrikova. "Before the General Reform of the Wholesale Price Structure," *Hospodarske Noviny* [Prague] (February 11, 1966).

22 Havelka, J. "The System of Management and Agriculture," *Zivot Strany* [Prague], 4 (1966).

23 Hronec, F. "New Measures on Price Policy," *Praca* [Bratislava] (November 9, 1965).

24 Klaus, V. and T. Jezek. "Fear of Inflation?" *Kulturni Tvorba* [Prague] (December 15, 1966).

25 Koctuch, H. "How and When to Invest," *Praca* (January 28, 1966).

26 Kostka, R. "We Need Prospering Enterprises," *Rude Pravo* (March 24, 1966).

27 Kovacik, J. "A Difficult Birth," *Praca* (December 21, 1965).

28 Kouril, F. "This Is also Cooperation," *Rude Pravo* (September 13, 1965).

29 Kozusnik, C. "Procrastination as a Planning Principle," *Reporter* [Prague] (July 16, 1966).

30 Kyprova, V. "The Role of World Prices in the New System of Management," *Planowane Hospodarstvi* [Prague], 10 (1966).

31 Lehar, L. "Let Us Learn a Lesson from Our Own Past," *Prace* [Prague] (August 17, 1966).

32 Loebl, E. "Possibilities and Problems," *Kulturny Zivot* [Bratislava] (January 20, 1967).

33 ———. "On Dogmatism in Economic Thinking," *Kulturny Zivot* (September 28 and October 12, 1963).

34 ———. "Not by Bread Alone," *Kulturni Zivot* (January 16, 1965).

35 ———. "Financial Plans and the Principles of Business Profitability," *Hospodarskie Noviny* (April 1, 1966).

36 Lipawski, J. "What Remuneration to Whom?" *Prace* (May 7, 1966).

37 "mlk." "Price Development in Perspective," *Svobodne Slovo* [Prague] (December 8, 1966).

38 Novak, O. "How the Wholesale Price System Is To Be Changed," *Rude Pravo* (December 29, 1965).

39 Reznicek, J. "The New System in 1966," *Rude Pravo* (December 22, 1965).

40 Sekera, J. "Agriculture under the Magnifying Glass," *Nova Mysl* [Prague] (August 9, 1966).

41 Selucky, R. "Technical Proficiency and Political Maturity," *Svobodne Slovo* (March 21, 1965).

42 ———. "The New System of Management Has Started," *Plamen* [Prague], 1 (1967).

43 ———. "The Cadres and the New System of Management," *Mlada Fronta* [Prague] (November 21, 1964).

44 ———. "People and Plan," *Kulturni Tvorba* (February 7, 1963).

45 Sik, O. "The Survivals of Dogmatism in Political Economy Must Be Overcome," *Nova Mysl*, 9 (1963).

46 ———. "The Future Demands and a Critical Review of the Past," *Kulturni Tvorba* (November 19, 1964).

47 ———. "The Problems Involved in the Transition to the New System," Pt I, *Rude Pravo* (February 18, 1966).

48 ———. "The Problems Involved in the Transition to the New System," Pt II, *Rude Pravo* (February 22, 1966).

49 ———. "The Problems Involved in the Transition to a New System," Pt III, *Rude Pravo* (February 23, 1966).

50 ———. "The Way to the New System Is Not an Easy One," interview in *Praca* (June 4, 1966).

51 ———. "On the Threshold of a New Stage in the Development of Socialist Economy," *Rude Pravo* (June 5, 1966).

52 ———. "What Is and What Is Not within the Possibilities of the New System," *Prace* (December 7, 1966).

53 Stejskal, E. "Present Tasks Demand High Qualifications," *Rude Pravo* (May 13, 1965).

54 Straka, M. "Big Tasks Demand Uncompromising Solutions," *Svobodne Slovo* (July 15, 1966).

55 Strougal, L. "On the Proposal for the Perfected System of Management in Agriculture," *Rude Pravo* (February 2, 1966).

56 Toman, J. "Socialist Planning—Socialist Enterprise," *Nova Mysl* (July 12, 1966).

57 Typolt, J. "Fixed, Flexible and Free Prices," *Rude Pravo* (November 25, 1965).

58 ———. "The Price System Reform Well under Way," *Vecerni Praha* [Prague] (June 3, 1966).

59 ———. "Wholesale and Retail Prices," *Rude Pravo* (September 22, 1966).

60 ——— and A. Novak. "The Principles of Reform of the Wholesale Price Structure," *Planovane Hospodarstvi*, 2 (1966).

61 Valouch, Z. "Will the Executive and Administrative Apparatus Grow?" *Rude Pravo* (July 19, 1966).

62 Vlasak, F. "Czechoslovak Industry under the New System of Management," *Czechoslovak Foreign Trade* [Prague], English Edition, 1 (1966).

63 Zajacova, V. "The Attitude of the Party to non-Party Specialists," *Pravda* [Bratislava] (January 30, 1966).

64 Unsigned. "On the Activity of Central Management Organs," *Rude Pravo* (November 4, 1965).

65 Unsigned. An interview with A. Hodulak—Deputy Chairman of the Union of Foundry Workers, *Prace* (June 10, 1966).

66 Unsigned. An interview with Prof. Liberman, "A Soviet Economist Talks About the New System of Management," *Prace* (July 26, 1966).

67 Unsigned. An interview with Deputy Minister of Agriculture, K. Vaclavu, *Rude Pravo* (August 24, 1966).

68 Unsigned. "The Unions Will Not Retreat Anymore," *Praca* (August 3, 1966).

69 Unsigned. "Assistance in the Change of Employment for Displaced Workers," *Praca* (December 25, 1966).

Official Documents and Statements

70 Resolution of the Presidium of the Central Committee of the CPCS, "The Proposal Concerning Principles for Perfecting the Planned Direction of the National Economy," *Rude Pravo* (October 17, 1964).

71 Resolution of the Central Committee of the CPCS, "Concerning the Main Trend in Perfecting the Planned Direction of National Economy, and on Party Work," *Rude Pravo* (January 30, 1965).

72 Decision of the Presidium of the Central Committee of the CPCS, "About the Cadre Work," *Zivot Strany*, 2 (January 1965).

73 J. Hendrych's speech of the January 1965 Central Committee meeting, "The Work and the Task of the Party and Other Social Organizations," *Rude Pravo* (February 3, 1965).

74 Resolution of the Central Committee of the CPCS, "Concerning the Activities of the Organs of Central Management," *Rude Pravo* (November 4, 1965).

75 Interview with Premier J. Lenart, *Rude Pravo* (January 23, 1966).

76 D. Kolder's speech at the Congress of the Society for Science and Technology, *Rude Pravo* (March 4, 1966).

77 Resolution of the Central Committee of the CPCS, "On the Main Trends of the Improvement of Planned Management in Agriculture," *Rude Pravo* (March 24, 1966).

78 Resolution of the 13th Plenary Session of the Central Council of Trade Unions, *Prace* (April 28, 1966).

79 M. Pastyrik's speech at the 13th Congress of the CPCS, "Trade Unions under New Conditions," *Rude Pravo* (June 4, 1966).

80 Resolution of the 13th Congress of the CPCS, "For Further

All-Round Development of our Socialist Society," *Rude Pravo* (June 7, 1966).
81 Resolution of the Council of Ministers of the CSSR, "General Conditions of Enterprise Management Effective on 1 January 1966," *Hospodarskie Noviny*, special supplement (July 29, 1966).
82 Excerpts from the proposal of the Council of Ministers of CSSR, "On the Principles of the Perfected System of Planning and Management in Agriculture," *Socialisticke Zemedelstvi* [Prague], 8 (August 1966).
83 M. Pastyrik's speech at the Trade Union Congress in Prague, "About the Tasks of the Revolutionary Trade Union Movement in Securing a further Development of the Socialist Society," *Prace* (February 1, 1967).

Secondary Sources

84 V. Holesovsky, "Czechoslovakia's Economic Debate," *East Europe* (December 1964).
85 H. G. Shaffer, "Czechoslovakia's New Course," *Problems of Communism* (September–October 1965).

EAST GERMANY

Articles and periodicals

86 Rheinhold, G. "The Plan—A Decisive Instrument of Economic Policy," *Einheit* [East Berlin], 8 (August 1965).
87 Mann, H. "The Price under the Conditions of Technical Revolution," *Einheit*, 12 (December 1965), 76–84.
88 Ambree, K. and H. Mann. "Varying Prices in the System of Economic Levers," *Einheit*, 9 (September 1966), 1128–37.
89 Beetherr, M. "Four Price Types," *Ekonomicheska Gazieta* [Moscow], 40 (October 1966).

Official Documents and Statements

90 Resolution of the July 1963 Plenum of the Central Committee of the SED, "Guidelines on the New System of Economic Planning and the Direction of the National Economy," *Neues Deutschland* [East Berlin] (July 17, 1963).
91 Resolution of the May 1965 Plenum of the Central Committee of the SED, *Neuer Weg* [East Berlin], 12 (May 25, 1965), 641–47.

92 Ulbricht's speech at the December 1965 Plenum of the Central Committee of the SED, *Neues Deutschland* (December 18, 1965).

Secondary Sources

93 W. Berger, "The New Economic System in the GDR—Its Essence and Its Problems," *World Marxist Review* (February 1965).
94 D. Miller and H. G. Trend, "Economic Reforms in East Germany," *Problems of Communism* (March–April 1966).

HUNGARY

Articles and periodicals

95 Alle, P. "The Role of Private Plots," *Figyelo* [Budapest] (November 11, 1964).
96 Beckl, S. "Enterprise Democracy in the New System of Economic Management," *Partelet* [Budapest], 8 (August 1965).
97 ———. "The Reform of the Economic Mechanism and the Trade Unions," *Munka* [Budapest] (August 1966).
98 Bocz, S. "The Economic Mechanism and the Human Being," *Nepszabadsag* [Budapest] (April 29, 1966).
99 Csikos-Nagy B. "The 1968 Price Reform," *Figyelo* (April 13, 1966).
100 Csizmadia E. and S. Zsarnoczai. "Price Policy—A Key Problem," *Szabad Fold* [Budapest] (January 29, 1967).
101 Farago, J. "According to Work," *Nepszabadsag* (June 29, 1963).
102 Fock, J. "The Economic Reform Was Initiated by the Party and It Must Be Carried Out under the Leadership of the Party," *Nepszabadsag* (December 1, 1966).
103 ———. "On the Economic Tasks in 1966, on the New Five-Year-Plan and on the Measures Affecting the Wages and Prices in the Coming Year," *Nepszabadsag* (December 19, 1965).
104 Földeaki," B. "New Methods of Planning in the Farmers Cooperatives," *Szabad Fold* (September 6, 1965).
105 Gaspar, S. "In the Interest of the Society—In the Interest of the Working Man," *Nepszava* (August 14, 1966), 3.
106 ———. "The Work of Trade Unions Must be Broadened to Include New Elements," *Nepszabadsag* (December 2, 1966).
107 Horvath, L. "Growing Income—More Independent Management," *Veszpremi Naplo* [Veszprem county] (February 20, 1966).

108 K., A. "The Right of Veto," *Bekes Megyei Nepujsag* [Bekescsaba county] (December 11, 1966).

109 Keseru, J. "Management and Agriculture," *Nepszabadsag* (February 25, 1967).

110 Komocsin, L. "On the Standard of Living," *Nepszabadsag* (December 25, 1965).

111 Lakos, G. "The Reform of the Economic Mechanism in Agriculture," *Novgrad* [Novgrad county] (September 28, 1966).

112 Mate, G. "Confidence Is the Answer to the Plain Speech," *Nepszabadsag* (March 16, 1962).

113 Nyers, R. "Our Economy is Unbalanced," *Nepszabadsag* (March 13, 1966).

114 ———. "Reform of Economic Mechanism in Hungary," *Beke es Szocializmus* [Budapest] (October 1966).

115 Pirityi, O. "Our Economic Reform and Public Opinion—How Shall I Profit from It," *Tarsadalmi Szemle* [Budapest] (January 1967).

116 Somosköi, G. "Greater Independence—Greater Responsibility," *Nepszava* [Budapest] (August 7, 1966), 2.

117 ———. "The Growing Tasks of Trade Union Committees," *Partelet*, 10 (October 1966).

118 Soter, E. "Democracy in Enterprise," *Nepszabadsag*" (December 21, 1966).

119 Tar, J. "Along the Road to Further Development of Land Ownership," *Tarsadalmi Szemle*, 1 (January 1967), 25–31.

120 Wilcsek, J. "The Rate of Profit in the Management of Factories," *Tarsadalmi Szemle* (March 1965).

121 Unsigned. "Why Do We Support Private Plots," *Nepszabadsag* (November 15, 1963).

122 Unsigned. "Summary of Debates Concerning Enterprise Independence and Central Management," *Nepszabadsag* (December 25, 1965).

123 Unsigned. "The Council of Trade Unions Debates the Guidelines of a New Economic System," *Nepszava* (February 27, 1966).

124 Unsigned. "New Fuel Prices will Take Effect on April 1, 1966," *Nepszabadsag* (March 23, 1966).

125 Unsigned. "Party Guidance of Trade Unions," *Partelet*, 7 (July 1966), 20–25.

126 Unsigned. "The Increased Role and Tasks of the Trade Unions in Our Country," *Tarsadalmi Szemle*, 9 (September 1966).

127 Unsigned. "Meeting of the National Council of Trade Unions," *Nepszava* (October 1, 1966).
128 Unsigned. "On the Solution of the Problem of Manpower Policy in the Coalmining Industry," *Nepszabadsag* (March 5, 1967).

Official Documents and Statements

129 Statement by Sandor Gaspar, *Nepszabadsag* (June 19, 1966).
130 "Resolution of the Central Committee of the HSWP Concerning the Reform of Economic Mechanism," *Supplement to MTI's Weekly Bulletin* [Budapest], 2 (June 9, 1966).
131 Interview with Tivadar Nemeslaky, "The Reform of the Trade Unions and the Economic Mechanism," *Nepszabadsag* (October 16, 1966).
132 J. Kadar's speech at the 9th Congress of the HSWP, *Nepszabadsag* (December 2, 1966).
133 J. Kadar's closing speech at the 9th Congress of the HSWP, *Nepszabadsag* (December 4, 1966).

Secondary Sources

134 Sandor Kiss, "Hungary's Economic Situation," *East Europe* (May 1965).
135 "*La Riforma Economica in Ungheria e i Problemi della Democracia Socialista*" (economic reform in Hungary and the problems of socialist democracy), an interview with György Lukacs, *L'Unita* [Rome] (August 28, 1966).
136 Joseph Held, "Hungary—Iron out of Wood," *Problems of Communism* (November–December 1966), 37–43.
137 F. Bertone, "*L'Ungheria alle Soglie della Svolta Economica*" (Hungary and the threshold of economic changeover), *Rinascita* [Rome], 50 (December 17, 1966).

POLAND

Articles and periodicals

138 "AR," "Increased Tasks and Prerogatives of the Planning Commission," *Trybuna Ludu* [Warsaw] (January 5, 1960).
139 Bober, A. "Changed Titles—or the Impasse in Economic Organization," *Zycie Warszawy* [Warsaw] (October 26, 1965).
140 Bobrowski, Cz. "Before the Change in the Economic Model," *Zycie Gospodarcze* [Warsaw] (May 12, 1957).

141 Bodnar, A. "Socialism in the Countryside," *Polityka* [Warsaw] (May 30, 1964).

142 Brus, W. "The Concept of Incentives Based on the Profit Motive," *Zycie Gospodarcze*, 25 (June 23, 1957).

143 ———. "Some General Remarks on the Changes in the System of Planning and Management," *Gospodarka Planowa*" [Warsaw], 11 (November 1966), 10–15.

144 ———. "On Certain Stipulations of Economic Progress," *Zycie Gospodarcze*, 45 (November 11, 1962).

145 ———. "About the Theory of a Socialist Enterprise," *Zycie Gospodarcze*, 3 (January 23, 1966).

146———. A series of five articles under the common title, "A Closer Look at the Yugoslav System," *Zycie Gospodarcze*, 1–5 (1957).

147 Chadzynski, H. "A Conference about Industrial Associations," *Zycie Warszawy* (May 7, 1966).

148 Cholaj, H. "Contracts as Instruments of Agricultural Policy," *Zycie Partii* [Warsaw], 8 (August 1966).

149 Fidelski, R. "System of Industrial Management in Yugoslavia," *Nowe Drogi* [Warsaw], 2 (February 1957), 102–17.

150 Flakierski, H. "Who, Where and Why," *Zycie Gospodarcze*, 30 (July 26, 1959).

151 Galeski, B. "Premises of the Transformation of Peasant Agriculture," *Ekonomista* [Warsaw], 6 (1965).

152 ———. "Prospects of Peasant Economy in Our Country," *Nowe Drogi*, 1 (January 1967), 106–17.

153 Iwanicki, W. "An Important Decision," *Trybuna Ludu* (April 3, 1965).

154 ———. "Free Grants or Credits," *Trybuna Ludu* (December 15, 1965).

155 Jedrychowski, S. "About the Effectiveness of Economic Incentives in our Economy," *Nowe Drogi*, 4 (April 1962), 6–7.

156 Kleer, J. "Across Five Countries—What Has Been Done," *Polityka* [Warsaw] (September 25, 1965).

157 Kraus, K. "A Dispute About Refrigerators," *Zycie Gospodarcze*, 6 (February 6, 1966).

158 Kwiatkowski, Z. "The Right Man in the Right Slot?" *Zycie Literackie* [Cracow] (August 21, 1966).

159 Lange, O. "How Do I Visualize the Polish Economic Model"—*Trybuna Ludu* (December 31, 1957).

160 ———. "From Balances to Optimal Choice," *Nowe Drogi*, 2 (February 1965), 39–45.

161 Lewicki, B. "Mr. Director—We Want to Educate You," *Trybuna Ludu* (February 10, 1964).

162 Lipinski, E. "The Model of Socialist Economy,"—*Nowe Drogi*, 12 (December 1956), 31–39.

163 ———. "Workers' Councils, Enterprises and Other Matters," *Zycie Gospodarcze*, 51–52 (December 22–29, 1957).

164 ———. "The Principles of the Reform—the Economic Functions of Enterprises and Associations," *Zycie Gospodarcze*, 20 (May 16, 1965).

165 ———. "Competition in a Socialist Economy" (a theoretical study of the New Economic Model), *Zycie Gospodarcze*, 14 (April 3, 1966).

166 Madej, Z. "How to Make our Economic Mechanism More Perfect," *Zycie Gospodarcze*, 36 (September 6, 1964).

167 Mieszczankowski, M. "The Evolution of the Character of Peasant Economy in the People's Poland," *Nowe Drogi*, 5 (May 1964), 20–36.

168 Mujzel, J. "The Prices and the Model," *Zycie Gospodarcze*, 17 (April 28, 1957).

169 Mysiak, M. "Directions of Perfecting the System of Planning and Management in the Light of the Decisions of the IV Party Congress," *Nowe Drogi*, 1 (January 1965), 73–80.

170 Pajestka, J. "Changes in the Planning and Management," *Zycie Warszawy* (October 18, 1964).

171 ———. Reply to a questionnaire on "The Role of the Market in a Planned Socialist Economy," *Nowe Drogi*, 2 (February 1967).

172 ———. "Some Factors Affecting the Acceleration of Economic Development of our Country," *Nowe Drogi*, 12 (December 1962).

173 Redlich, J. "Vitamin O," *Zycie Warszawy* (September 16, 1966).

174 Soldaczuk, J. "The Price System in Trade between Socialist Countries and the Problems of the Socialist International Division of Labor," *Ekonomista*, 1 (1966), 73–89.

175 Wolowczyk, A. "The Reality and the Utopia of Investment Financing," *Zycie Gospodarcze*, 7 (February 16, 1964).

176 Zielinski, J. "The Markets and the Consumers," *Zycie Gospodarcze*, 24 (June 15, 1958).

177 Unsigned. "The Economic Council Has Begun Its Work, the Main Task Being the Elaboration of the Polish Economic Model," *Trybuna Ludu* (February 10, 1957).

178 Unsigned. "New Prices of Coal, Electricity, and Gas," *Trybuna Ludu* (March 29, 1963).

179 Unsigned. "The Reform of Rents and the Introduction of Housing Allowances," *Trybuna Ludu* (August 14, 1965).

180 Unsigned. "The Most Responsible Man in the Management Setup," *Zycie Gospodarcze*, 17 (April 24, 1966).

181 Unsigned. "Polish-GDR Cooperation in the Border Regions," *Zycie Warszawy* (May 11, 1966).

182 Unsigned. "The Change in Prices of Certain Manufactured Goods and Food Products," *Trybuna Ludu* (July 13, 1966).

183 Unsigned. "Changes in the Methods of Managing the Economy," *Trybuna Ludu* (January 7, 1967).

184 Unsigned. "Incomes in the Countryside and in the Towns," *Zycie Gospodarcze*, 8 (February 19, 1967).

Official Documents and Statements

185 Gomulka's speech at the VIII Central Committee Plenum of the PUWP, *Nowe Drogi*, (October 1956).

186 "The Guidelines of the Central Committee of the PUWP and of the Executive Committee of the United Peasant Party Concerning the Agricultural Policy," *Trybuna Ludu* (January 9, 1957).

187 "Theses of the Economic Council Concerning Certain Changes in the Economic Model," *Zycie Gospodarcze*, 22 (June 2, 1957).

188 "Theses of the Economic Council in the Matter of Determining the Principles of Price Structure," *Zycie Gospodarcze*, 51 (December 22–29, 1957).

189 The Report of the Politburo of the PUWP, "The Key Problem of the Economic Plan for 1964," *Nowe Drogi*, 12 (December 1963), 3–57.

190 "Theses of the Central Committee of the PUWP for the IV Party Congress," a pamphlet published by *Ksiazka i Wiedza* (March 1964), 111–15.

191 The Resolution of the IV Congress of the PUWP, *Trybuna Ludu* (June 25, 1964).

192 Decree No. 224 issued by the Council of Ministers of July 29, 1964, "Concerning the Economic Progress in National Economy and the Organization of Economic Services," *Monitor Polski* [Warsaw] (August 18, 1964).

193 S. Jedrychowski's speech at the IV Plenum of the Central Committee of the PUWP, *Trybuna Ludu* (July 27, 1965).

194 The Report of the Politburo of the PUWP presented at the IV Plenum of the Central Committee, "Directions of the Changes

in the System of Planning and Management of National Economy in the Years 1966–1970," *Nowe Drogi,* 8 (August 1965), 3–58.

195 "The Resolution of the IV Plenum of the Central Committee of the PUWP," *Nowe Drogi,* 8 (August 1965), 82–99.

Secondary Sources

196 W. Wende and A. Erlich, "The National Management Training Center in Warsaw," *International Labor Review* [Geneva], 5, (May 1965).

197 F. Lewis, *A Case History of Hope.* New York 1958.

198 K. Syrop, *Spring in October.* London, 1958.

Books published in Poland

199 Brus, W. *General Questions Concerning the Functioning of Socialist Economy.* State Scientific Publications [PWN] Warsaw, 1961.

200 Fick, B. *Economic Incentives in Industry.* State Economic Publications [PWE] Warsaw, 1965, pp. 54–69.

201 Gordon, J. *The Economics of an Industrial Enterprise,* a collection of analytical essays edited by J. Gordon. State Economic Publications. Warsaw, 1965.

202 Lange, O. *Theory of Production and Accumulation.* State Scientific Publications. Warsaw, 1961.

203 ———. *Optimal Decisions.* State Scientific Publications. Warsaw, 1964.

204 Plocica, A. *The Basis of Prices of Investment Goods.* State Economic Publications. Warsaw, 1964.

RUMANIA

Articles and periodicals

205 Agachi, N. "The Caliber of Enterprise Management," *Romania Libera* [Bucharest] (September 28, 1966).

206 Bituleanu, J. "The Profitability of Enterprises," *Probleme Economice* [Bucharest] (October 1966), 64–66.

207 Olteanu, J. "Is There a Science of Organization and Management," *Contemporanul* [Bucharest] (November 18, 1966).

208 Petrescu, L. "The Ability to Make Optimal and the Most Objective Decisions," *Romania Libera* (September 14, 1966).

209 Serban, B. "Enterprise Management in Step with Progress," *Romania Libera* (September 7, 1966).

Official Documents and Statements

210 The speech of Nikolae Ceausescu, *Scanteia* [Bucharest] (December 25, 1966).

SOVIET UNION

Articles and periodicals

211 Birman, A. "Inevitability," *Literaturna Gazieta* [Moscow], 2 (January 11, 1967).
212 Garbuzov, V. "Finances and Economic Stimuli," *Ekonomicheska Gazieta* [Moscow] (October 13, 1965).
213 Kantorovich, L. V. "The Development of Mathematical Methods of Economic Analysis," *Bulletin of the Academy of Sciences of USSR* [Moscow], 10 (1966), 5–14.
214 Kolesnev, S., M. Sokolov, and I. Suslov. "On the Problem of the Plan and the Market," *Selskaya Zhizn* [Moscow] September 22, 1966).
215 Liberman, J. G. "The Plan, Profits and Premium," *Pravda* [Moscow] (September 9, 1962).
216 Sitnin, V. "Price Is an Important Tool of Economic Management," *Pravda* (November 12, 1965).
217 ———. "The Economic Reform and the Review of Wholesale Prices for Industrial Products," *Kommunist* [Moscow], 14 (1966).
218 Unsigned. "Result of the Work of 43 Enterprises," *Ekonomicheska Gazieta*, 19 (1966).
219 Unsigned. "Strengthen the Labor Discipline," *Trud* [Moscow] (August 10, 1966).
220 Unsigned. "Unity of Words and Deeds," *Pravda* (October 2, 1966).
221 Unsigned. "The Confident Stride of the New Reform," *Pravda* (January 4, 1967).

Official Documents and Statements

222 N. S. Khrushchev's speech at November 1962 Plenum of the Central Committee of the CPSU, *Pravda* (November 20, 1962).
223 A. N. Kosygin's report to September 1965 Plenum of the Central Committee of the CPSU, "On Improving the Management of

Industry, Perfecting Planning and Increasing the Economic Incentives for Industrial Production," *Pravda* (September 28, 1965).

224 "The Statute of the Socialist Production Enterprise," *Ekonomicheska Gazieta* (October 20, 1965).

Secondary Sources

225 Marshall I. Goldman, "Economic Controversy in the Soviet Union," *Foreign Affairs* (April 1963).

226 A. Nove, "Soviet National Income Statistics," *Soviet Studies* (January 1955), 259–60.

227 David H. Eving, "The Russian Yearns for the Managerial Mind," *Harper's Magazine* (January 1965).

228 "*Der Gewinn Muss Entrostet Werden*" (the profit must be cleared of rust), an interview with Prof. Liberman, *Industriekurier* [Düsseldorf] (May 6, 1965).

YUGOSLAVIA

Articles and periodicals

229 Bajec, M. and P. Stojanovic. "The Logic and the Absurdity of Work Stoppages," *Borba* [Belgrade] (October 16, 1966).

230 Bakaric, V. "Basic Economic Stimulus Must Be the Working Man," *Vjesnik* [Zagreb] (April 4, 1965), 2–3.

231 Brkic, J. "Remarks on Earnings and Working Conditions," *Borba* (October 12, 1966).

232 Grlickov, A. "What Type of Foreign Investments," a press conference by Grlickov, a member of the Federal Executive Council (Government), *Borba* (March 17, 1967), 1 and 16.

233 Kovacevic, B. "Unemployed and Over-employed," *Vjesnik* (January 26, 1967).

234 Krmpotic, N. "A Contemporary on Strikes," *Vjesnik* (November 10, 1966).

235 Mimica, M. "Greediness or Necessity—Why People Go Abroad" *Polityka* [Belgrade] (January 30, 1966), 9.

236 Stojanovic, P. "The Departure of our Workers for Abroad Cannot be Prevented by Administrative Measures," *Borba* (October 20, 1965), 5.

237 ———. "About 100,000 Workers Abroad via Labor Exchange Office," *Borba* (December 23, 1966).

238 ———. "On the Eve of the Assembly Debate on Work Stoppages," *Borba* (January 12, 1967).

239 Vucovic, D. "The Pressure Eases Up," *Borba* (October 20, 1965), 5.

240 Vukmanovic-Tempo, S. "The Trade Unions and Economic Planning," *Yugoslav Trade Unions* [Belgrade], English edition (July 1966).

241 Unsigned. "The Phenomenon Called a Work Stoppage," *Ekonomska Politika* [Belgrade] (April 11, 1964), 565.

242 Unsigned. "Economic Reforms Begin to Operate," *Borba* (July 25, 1965).

243 Unsigned. "What the Economic Reform Will Change," *Komunist* [Belgrade] (July 29, 1965), 3.

244 Unsigned. "Employment Outside Yugoslavia," *Ekonomska Politika* (October 15, 1966), 1320.

245 Unsigned. "Yugoslavs Abroad," *Yugoslav Trade Unions*, English edition, 2 (1967), 7–8.

Official Documents and Statements

246 Tito's speech, "Better Living Conditions and Higher Living Standards Would Make Possible a Better Development of our Economy," *Politika* (April 21, 1964).

247 "Resolution of the VIII Congress Concerning the Future Tasks of the League of Communists of Yugoslavia," *Borba* (December 15, 1964), 1–3.

248 E. Kardelj, "From Self-Managing Interest of the Workers Toward the Integration of Regional and National Interests," *Ekonomska Politika* (November 27, 1965), 1562–65.

249 Krajger's speech at the joint session of Federal and Economic Chambers of the Yugoslav Parliament, *Borba* (December 29, 1965).

250 Resolution of the III Plenum of the Central Committee of the League of Yugoslav Communists, *Borba* (March 13, 1966).

251 Proceedings of the III Plenum of the Central Committee of the League of Yugoslav Communists, *Borba* (March 14, 1966).

252 Krajgerś exposé in Parliament, a supplement to *Borba* (July 25, 1966).

253 "Better Conditions and Treatment for our Workers about to be Secured Through Agreements," an official statement by Tanjug, Borba (February 5, 1967).

GENERAL AREA

Secondary Sources

254 C. Zoerb, "The Performance of the Private and Public Sector in Bloc Agriculture," *Radio Free Europe Research Papers* [Munich] (January 1965).

255 US Department of Agriculture, "The USSR and East European Agricultural Situation" (March 1966).

256 H. Trend, "The New Residual Claimant Wage System in Eastern Europe," *Radio Free Research Papers* (April 28, 1966).

ADDENDUM (articles located since the book has gone to press)

I. R., "The Relationship of Wages and the Cost of Living," *Zemedelskie Noviny* [Prague] (December 23, 1966).

J. Szpt, "The Time of Reckoning," *Zycie Warszany* (August 19, 1964).

SUBJECT INDEX

NAME INDEX

Michael Gamarnikow is Assistant Director, Polish Broadcasting Department in Radio Free Europe. He received his diploma in economics and applied statistics from the University of Glasgow, and his B. Sc. (Econ.) honors degree from the University of London.

The manuscript was edited by Robert H. Tennenhouse. The book was designed by Edgar Frank. The typeface used for display is Bodoni originally designed by Giambatista Bodoni in the late 18th century. The text face is Linotype Janson cut originally by Anton Janson in the late 17th century.

The book is printed on S. D. Warren's Olde Style Antique paper and bound in Columbia Bayside Vellum cloth. Manufactured in the United States of America.